CFA level 1: 2022

Economics

Complete economics in one week

M. Imran Ahsan

Preface

This is my 4th book on CFA level 1. CFA 2022.

CFA 2019 Financial Reporting and Analysis, Economics for CFA level 1 2019 were highly appreciated and for that I am much obliged. Actually the succession of those books made me to take one step ahead and I wrote this book.

I am happy to launch this book with which you can cover and master your Economics part of CFA level 1 with great ease. Nevertheless this is most affordable and quality study material.

I am looking forward to come up with more books. Love you all the aspirants and may you succeed in your goals.

M. Imran Ahsan
Ch.imranahsen@gmail.com
Whats app# 00923465006818

Contents

Tittle

Preface 2

Study Session 3 4

Economics (1) 4

READING 8: TOPICS IN DEMAND AND SUPPLY
ANALYSIS 4

READING 9: THE FIRM AND MARKET STRUCTURES 42

READING 10: AGGREGATE OUTPUT, PRICES, AND
ECONOMIC GROWTH 90

READING 11: UNDERSTANDING BUSINESS CYCLES ..130

Study Session 4 154

READING 12: MONETARY AND FISCAL POLICY 154

READING 13: INTERNATIONAL TRADE AND CAPITAL
FLOWS 193

READING 14: CURRENCY EXCHANGE RATES 215

Study Session 3
Economics (1)

READING 8: TOPICS IN DEMAND AND SUPPLY ANALYSIS

LOS 8a: Calculate and interpret price, income, and cross-price elasticities of demand and describe factors that affect each measure.

Price elasticity of demand: Also called own price elasticity of demand.

It is "percentage change in quantity demand of a commodity (Goods or services) due to percentage change in its own price.

Price elasticity of demand shows responsiveness of quantity demand to change in price.

Formula;

Own price elasticity= (%
change in Quantity demand) /(% change in price$)$

We can also write it as

$$E^p = \frac{\left(\frac{\Delta QD}{Qd}\right)x100}{\left(\frac{\Delta p}{p}\right)x100} = \frac{\Delta Qd/Qd}{\Delta p/p} = \frac{\Delta Qd}{\Delta p} \times \frac{P}{Qd} = \frac{\Delta Qd}{Qd} \div \frac{\Delta p}{p}$$

Where E^p = Own price elasticity of demand

ΔQd = change in quantity demand

Δp= Change in price

P= Initial price

Qd= Initial quantity demand.

Let`s solve an hypothetical example

Price of Hamburger	Quantity demanded
1$	10

2$	4

In above table it is shown that when the price of Hamburger is 1$ its demand is 10 units. Price increased to 2$ and the quantity demanded is reduced to only 4.

Put this data into our price elasticity formula;

$$E^p = \frac{\Delta Qd}{Qd} \div \frac{\Delta p}{p} = \frac{4 - 10}{10} \div \frac{2 - 1}{1} = \frac{-6}{10} \div \frac{1}{1} = -0.6$$

Interpretation: The negative sign (normally we get – sign in own price elasticity) shows inverse relationship between Qd and price. It means when price increases the Qd decreases and vice versa.

0.6 means when price changes 1 percent, the Qd will change by 0.6% (in opposite direction as we have negative sign).

Own price elasticity can be one from the following

Elastic demand: E^p **>1.** When demand respond more than the price (in %) we say the demand is highly elastic. In this case the answer to the price elasticity formula is higher than one.

Note: When we are talking about E^p <>=1 we ignore negative sign. So if we get -5 we consider it as 5 and we know that 5 is greater than one. Same way −o.6 is actually 0.6 which is less than one.

Elasticity would be greater than one normally in case of luxury commodities. It means demand changes more than price. If there is a small increase in price, demand for luxury goods decrease substantially. On the other hand if there is a small decrease in price the demand will increase substantially. Examples of luxuries are yacht, jewelry etc.

Less elastic/ Inelastic demand: E^p**<1.** When Qd is less responsive to a price change, demand is called inelastic. In this case the answer to the formula would be less than one.

Normally Elasticity is less than one in case of necessities. Necessities are those goods which are essential for living like water, flour, clothes etc. in this case when price increases substantially there is less decrease in demand.

Equal Elastic demand/ unitary elastic demand: $E^p = 1$

When there is same percentage change in price and Qd the demand would be equally elastic. In this case the answer to the price elasticity of demand would be one.

Normally Elasticity is equal to one in case of comforts. Comforts are the goods which are not critical for life but bring comfort into life (not luxuries). For example high quality food (in relation to normal food which is necessity). These goods are placed in between luxury and necessities.

Perfectly inelastic demand: $E^p=0$ When Qd does not respond at all to the change in price, Demand is called perfectly inelastic. This is extreme case. It can happen in serious crisis like war or droughts.

An example of perfectly inelastic demand: At all the values of P there is no change in Q.

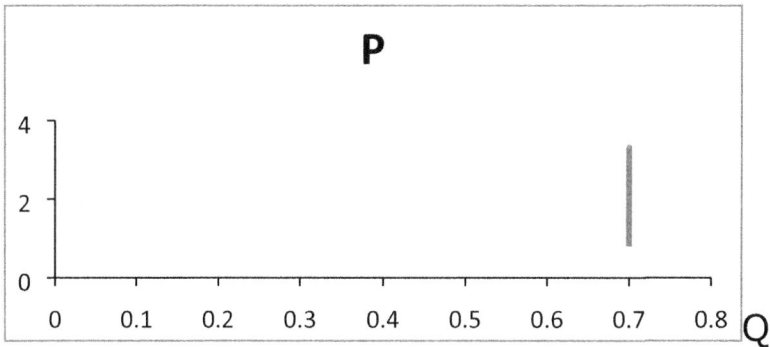

An Example of perfectly elastic demand (Elasticity = ∞) quantity of demand changes infinitely while p remains same as shown in following figure.

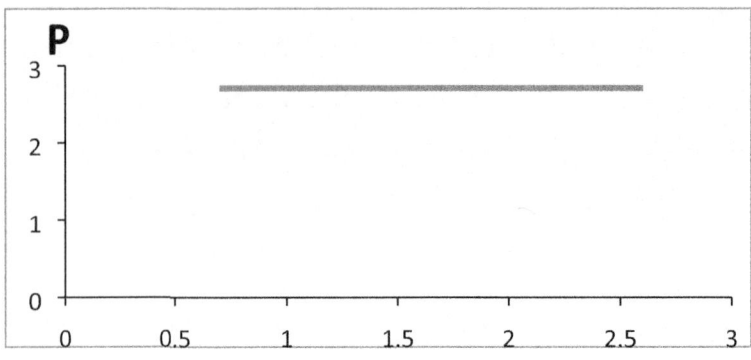

Factors affecting Elasticity:

There are many factors which can affect elasticity as follows.

Availability of substitutes: Fewer or not availability of substitute goods cause inelastic demand and vice versa. For example if we have only one gasoline station in our city, an increase in price of gasoline by that station would not make any decrease in the purchase of gasoline. On the other hand if there are two gasoline stations providing same quality gasoline. If one of them increases its price the customers will move towards other station.

Portion of expenditures on that good: Larger the portion of income is spent on a specific good more elastic the demand would be. If the small portion of income is spent on a good the elasticity tends to be less. For example increase in price of toothpaste by 10 percent has least affect on purchasing.

Time: Greater the time available to respond for a price change, elasticity tends to be greater. For example if there is an increase in price of gasoline, consumers initially make adjustments in other expenditures (and do not cut the gasoline demand) but as time passes, they tends to buy fuel efficient cars, so the demand for gasoline decreases.

Elasticity on linear demand curve:

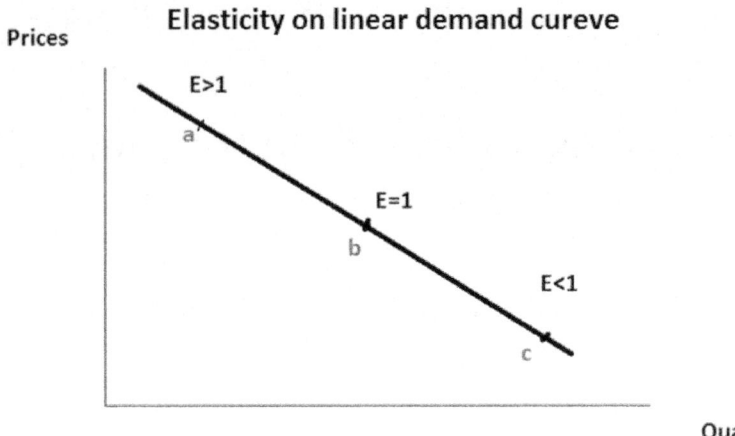

Prices

Elasticity on linear demand cureve

E>1

a

E=1

b

E<1

c

Quantity

As shown in above figure, Elasticity is higher on a point above from midpoint of linear demand curve. Elasticity is equal to one at exactly center. When we move down from midpoint elasticity is less than 1. So it does not remain same in linear demand curve. One important point here, do not confuse elasticity with change in prices and quantity. The change in price and quantity make the slope of demand curve while the elasticity is percentage change in both.

When the elasticity is greater than one (there will be substantial percentage change in demand as price changes little) firms do not increase the price of their product. This is because if they increase the prices even 1% there would be more than 1% decrease in demand. So their total revenues (price x Quantity) will decrease.

When E=1 there is no need to change the price. When we increase prices by 5% there will be a decrease in Qd by 5% so as a result the Total revenues will remain same.

When E<1. Firms will get benefits by increasing prices as the demand will not respond much to an increase in price so their total revenues will increase.

Income elasticity of demand

Income is also a factor which can affect demand. Income elasticity is the calculation of sensitivity of demand to changes in income.

E^y = percentage change in Qd due to percentage change in income

$$E^y = \frac{\Delta Qd}{Qd} \div \frac{\Delta y}{y}$$

Y is symbol of income

E^y is income elasticity

Δy = change in income

Y is original income

Example

Income (Y) $	Qd (liters)
10000	20
12000	25

By putting values in our formula

$$E^y = \frac{25 - 20}{20} \div \frac{12000 - 10000}{10000} = \frac{5}{20} \div \frac{2000}{10000} =$$

$$0.25 \div 0.2 = \mathbf{1.25}$$

For normal products income and quantity demanded has positive relationship. As income increases consumers tend to buy more and vice versa. It means with income elasticity we would have positive answer.

Normal goods are defined as the goods which are bought more as income increases.

The goods which consumers buy less with increase in income are _called inferior goods_. For inferior goods we will have negative income elasticity.

Crossed price elasticity of demand

Substitutes or complementary products also affect demand.

Substitutes are the products which can be used alternatively. Like Samsung and Sony mobile phones.

Complementary products are the products which can only be used if used together. For example left foot shoe and right foot shoe, milk and tea.

Cross price elasticity is the calculation of sensitivity of demand of one commodity to changes in the prices of substitutes or complementary products.

$$E^{ab} = \frac{\Delta Qda}{Qda} \div \frac{\Delta Pb}{Pb}$$

ΔQda = Qd of a product.

ΔPb = Change in price of product b

Lets solve an example of substitute goods for Coca cola and Pepsi

Price of Coca cola	Qd (coca cola)	Price of Pepsi	Qd of Pepsi
1$	200	1$	200
2$	30	1$	370

We can see that when price of Coca Cola increases, there is close substitute of Pepsi is available to customers. So most of the consumers moved towards Pepsi even there is no change in Pepsi price. Ok now we will calculate cross price elasticity of Coca cola to Pepsi as

$$E^{ab} = \frac{\Delta Qd(pepsi)}{Qd\ (pepsi)} \div \frac{\Delta P(Coca\ cola)}{P(Coca\ cola)}$$

$$E^{ab} = \frac{370 - 200}{200} \div \frac{2 - 1}{1} = 0.85$$

In case of substitute good the price of one commodity increases, the demand for its substitute increases as we would have cheaper alternative available to us. So, for substitute products we have positive elasticity.

When goods are complementary the increase in price of one commodity will cause a decrease in demand for other commodity because the combined price of the two complementary products together has risen. So in this case we will have negative elasticity.

Calculation of elasticity is not always that simple

Let's solve following examples when elasticity is to be calculated from demand function.

Demand function shows negative relationship between demand and price.

Following is demand function for gasoline
$Qd = 500 - 2p$
Calculate price elasticity of Gasoline at price of 5$ per gallon.

From this data we know that p is 3 and we can calculate Qd as

Qd = 500- 2(3) =494
  We know that

$$E^P = \frac{\Delta Qd}{\Delta p} \times \frac{P}{Qd}$$

The slope of demand function is -2 which is $\frac{\Delta Qd}{\Delta p}$
By putting our values in our elasticity formula
E^P *= -2 x (3/494) = -0.012. This is highly inelastic demand.*

Income elasticity and cross price elasticity can also be calculated same way.

We assume the values of independent variables except the variable we need to calculate the elasticity.

Following is the demand function of an individual
QDpet = 5000 – 2Ppet + 0.5y + 0.60CNG – 0.0.12 P auto

This is a complex demand function in which demand for Petrol is negative function of its own price while is positive   function of income (Y), substitute (CNG, the compressed natural gas another fuel for cars) and also negative function of complementary good (price auto car).

Calculate Income Elasticity

Assuming price of petrol 5\$/gallon, price of CNG 2\$/kg and price of auto 20000\$, calculate income elasticity of demand.
Look closely we have assumed all values except income as it is the variable of our interest.

Put all value in our demand function we have
Qd = 5000 – 2(5) + 0.5y + 0.60(2) – 0.12(20000)
Qd= 2591.24+ 0.5y

For income of 10000\$ the Qd is
Qd= 2591.24 + 0.5(10000) =7591.24

Formula for income elasticity is

$$E^y = \frac{\Delta Qd}{Qd} \div \frac{\Delta y}{y} \quad or$$

$$E^y = \frac{\Delta Qd}{Qd} \times \frac{y}{\Delta y} \quad or$$

$$E^y = \frac{\Delta Qd}{\Delta y} \times \frac{y}{Qd}$$

And we know that slope of

income ($\frac{\Delta Qd}{\Delta y}$) is 0.5, income is 10000 and Qd is 7591.24

Put all these into our formula we get

$$E^y = 0.5 \times \frac{10000}{7591.24} = 0.658654$$

Interpretation: If income changes (increase or decreases) by one percent the demand will changes by 0.658654 percent in same direction as we have positive sign with income elasticity.

Same way we can calculate Cross Price elasticity. We know that petrol and CNG are alternative goods. So what will be effect of change in price of CNG on demand for Petrol? So now we have to replace everything`s value except CNG.

QDPet = 5000 – 2Ppet + 0.5y + 0.60CNG – 0.0.12 P auto
Using the same values except for CNG we can rewrite above function as follows
QDPet = 5000 – 2(5) + 0.5(10000) + 0.60(CNG) – 0.12(20000)
$\quad$ =5000 -10 + 5000+ 0.60CNG – 2400
$\quad$ Qdpet =7590 + 0.60CNG
For CNG price of 20$ the Qd is
Qdpet = 7602

Slope for CNG is 0.60 which means $\frac{\Delta QdPet}{\Delta PCNG}$ =0.60. By re arranging cross elasticity formula we have

$$E^{ab} = \frac{\frac{\Delta Qd(pet)}{Qd\ (pet)} \div \frac{\Delta P(CNG)}{P(CNG)} = \frac{\Delta Qd(pet)}{\Delta P(CNG)} \times \frac{Qd\ (pet)}{P(CNG)}}{}$$

Put all values

$$E^{ab} = \frac{0.60x\frac{7602}{20}}{} = 228.06$$

Interpretation: *When Price of CNG changes 1 percent the demand of Petrol will change 228.06% in same direction. Huge number of customers will move towards buying petrol if CNG owners will increase their price even a little bit. So the beast strategy for CNG owners is to decrease their price so the huge number of petrol customers move towards CNG.*

LOS 8b: Compare substitution and income effects.

Income effect: Changes in consumer`s equilibrium due to changes in his purchasing power is called income effect.

Normally when the price of a product increases its demand decreases and when the prices falls its demand increases. I said normally. This is true for normal products. Sometimes with a decrease in price of a product demand for that product also decreases and increase in the price increases its demand. This is the case of inferior/ or Giffen goods.

So the income effect can be positive or negative.

Substitution effect: change in consumer equilibrium due to changes in price of a product is known as substitution effect. When price of a product falls, it becomes relatively cheaper. So the consumer substitutes the dearer product with the cheaper one.

When price of a product falls it is also seen as increase in income because budget/ income line moves ahead and when price of a product increases it can also be seen as fall in income as income line moves backwards.

When price of a product **X** decreases we have one of the following outcome:

- Both substitution and income effects are positive the demand for product increases.

- Substitution effect is positive but income effect is negative (inferior product case) and
- Income effect is smaller than substitution effect the demand for product rises.
- Substitution effect is positive but income effect is negative and larger than substitution effect the demand for product x decreases.

Graphical presentation of these effects

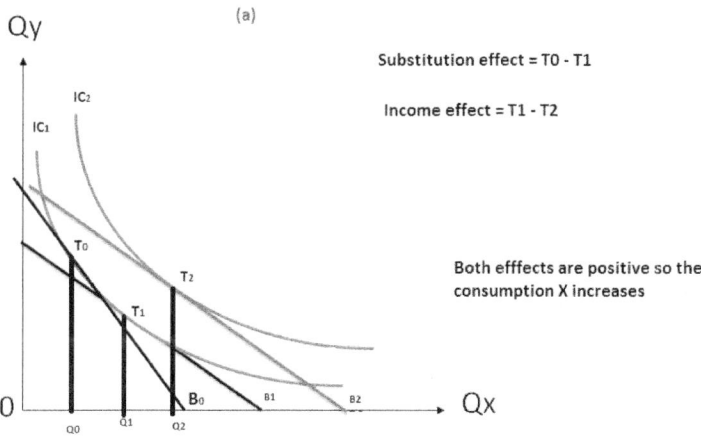

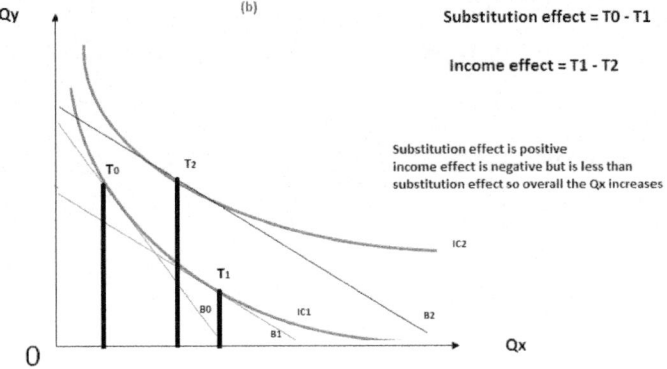

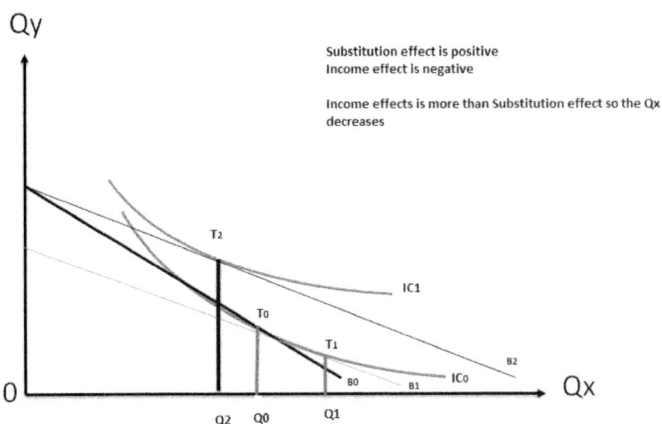

The initial budget line is B0. After fall in price of X the new budget line is B2.

B1 is new theoretical budget line on original IC0 (to show consumer`s preferred bundle) to show substitution effect from T0 to T1. T1 is the new preferred bundle by consumer as the price of X decreases and it is relatively cheaper now (but consumer`s utility is unchanged as he is on same IC) Remember that the substitution effect is always positive when price falls.

Income effect is T1 – T2, from old budget line and IC0 to New budget line and AC1.

In panel (a) both the income and substitution effects are positive so the consumption of Good X increases from Q0 to Q1.

In panel (b) the income effect is negative but smaller than substation effect so the Quantity of good X still increases (the increase in quantity of good X is less in panel (b) than from panel (a).

In panel (c) the law of demand is violated. As the price of good X falls the consumption of X decreases. This is because the income effect is negative and lager than substitution effect.

So the equilibrium quantity (Q1) is less than Q_0.

LOS 8c: Contrast normal goods with inferior goods.

Normal Goods: These are the goods for which income effect is positive as we discussed in panel (a) in previous Los.

Inferior goods are those for which income effect is negative as we have discussed in panel (b) and (c).

The Giffen goods are those inferior goods for which income effect is negative and outweighs the substitution effect as in panel (c) of previous LOS.

Giffen goods has upward sloped demand curve because when price falls their overall demand decrease

Substitution effect is always positive in all these three cases because when price Falls the good becomes cheaper.

One good can be normal good for some specific people and it could be superior for others. For example air travel can be superior good for low income people but are normal good for higher income people. A good can be normal for you if you have low income but it can be inferior when your income increases.

Driving your own car is normal good for middle income people while it's inferior for higher income people.

Veblen good: These goods are used as a symbol of status. When their price increases they become more desirable and their demand increases. This is true up to some extent. In a specific price range their demand increases with the increase in price. If this type of good exists, there must be a limit to the price otherwise the price would increase without limits. So the Veblen good are also having positive demand curve and it violate the law of demand. Some luxury goods like private jet travel come under this category.

LOS 8d: Describe the phenomenon of diminishing marginal returns.

First of all we need to understand some terminologies and concepts

Factors of production: These are the resources are inputs which a company uses to generate outputs.

Following are four factors of production

1 Land: It is the place where business operates.

2 Labor: It includes all skilled and unskilled people working for that business from labor to top management.

3 Capital: Capital means all manufacturing facilities like plant Machinery Tools and equipment.

4 Materials: Materials include the raw materials used for production. This material can be in raw form or output of other industries.

For economic analysis we normally take two factors of production into account like labor and capital. The output of a firm is a function of these inputs.

Short run time period: This is the time in which at least one factor of production for example capital is fixed. We can only increase our production by increasing units of labor, as labor can be changed easily in comparison to capital.

Marginal product/ return: This is the increase in production by employing 1 extra unit of labor while keeping the units of capital fixed. It can also be defined as change in the total production by changing unit of labor.

We can examine the marginal product of firm by increasing the units of labor. If every extra unit of labor (keeping the capital constant) gives us higher and higher marginal product, it is called **increasing marginal return**. It means, every next unit of labor gives us more marginal product than previous one. This happens when the workers co-ordinate with each other and causes substantial increase in the output.

This is the first stage of production process. At this stage the capital is adequate for the workers and total production is increasing with increasing rate.

After some specific point, adding one extra worker will gives us less marginal product than previous one. Remember that Total production is still increasing but at decreasing rate. This is the second stage of production known as **diminishing marginal return**.

After second stage there comes **negative marginal return**. It means adding extra units of labor gives us negative marginal return. At and after this point total production start falling.

Following table explains all these three stages.

Units of capital (K)	Units of labor (L)	Total production (TP)	Marginal production (MP)
10	1	100	100
10	2	220	120
10	3	350	130
10	4	450	100
10	5	500	50
10	6	510	10

10	7	500	-10
10	8	480	-20

As you can see in this table the units of capital are fixed to ten. First unit of labor gives 100 units of output. This is our first unit of labor, so marginal and total are same. Using second unit of labor give us marginal product of 120 units so the total production becomes 220 units. Up to the third unit of labor, marginal product increases and total product increases with increasing rate. By using 4th unit of labor, marginal product decreases. Still we have increase in the total product with decreasing rate. 7th and 8th unit of labor gives us negative marginal product and we experience a decrease in total product

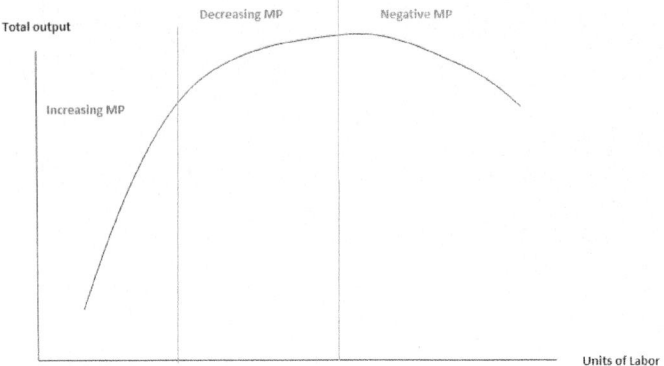

LOS 8e: Determine and interpret breakeven and shutdown points of production.

Short run time period: This is the time in which at least one factor of production for example capital is fixed. We can only increase our production by increasing units of labor, as labor can be changed easily in comparison to capital.

Long run time period: It is the time. In which all factors of production are variable a firm can change its production by increasing units of capital and units of labor.

All costs are variable in this time. For example a firm can increase its production by installing new plant and machinery, hiring new workers or it can reduce its cost by cutting down the plant and machinery.

Fixed cost: It is the cost which does not change as the production level changes. This is true up to some extent for example rent of factory building. Owner of the factory has to pay fixed amount of rent regardless he produces 1 unit or 100 units.

Variable cost: It is the cost which changes with the change in production level. For example cost of raw material. When we produce more units of shoes we need more leather so the cost of leather increases (so it is variable cost).

Total cost = variable cost +fixed cost

Average cost = Total cost / output

Average variable cost = variable cost / output

Average fixed cost = Fixed cost / output

We can discuss shut down and break even points under two conditions.;

1. Shutdown and break-even point under perfect competition.

2. Shut down and break-even point under imperfect competition.

Perfect competition is the situation in the market in which there are very large number of buyers and sellers and no one can affect the prevailing prices individually.

Imperfect competition: It is the market situation in which characteristics of perfect competition are not fulfilled. In this type of market structure there are many buyers but sellers are less than buyers. Depending on the degree of competition sellers have control over prices. Imperfect market structures include monopoly (with single seller) monopolistic competition (with many sellers) etc.

In coming LOS we will discuss these structures in detail.

Total revenues are price times quantity sold. TR = PxQ.

Average revenues = TR/Q

Marginal revenues = change in TR by producing one extra output.

Shutdown and break-even point under perfect competition

Under perfect competition Average revenues = TR/Q = P =AR =MR

In short run time period if firm is covering its variable cost it should operate to minimize the cost. It means price is just enough to cover variable costs. If price is below than average variable cost then the firm should shut down temporarily (in short run).

In long run if price is less than its average total cost it should shut it down.

Break even and shout down points by using marginal revenues and marginal cost approach.

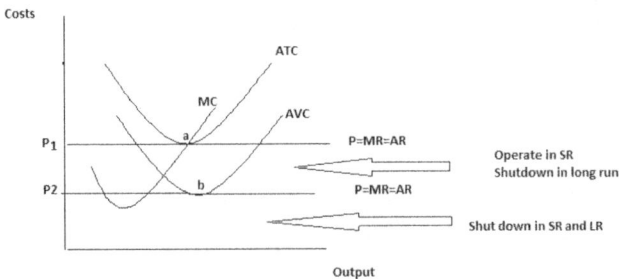

At point "a" the price P1 is just covering all costs so it is the breakeven point. At this point and above the firm should operate in short run and in long run. In the area below point "a" the firm should operate in SR as it is at least covering its variable cost. Below point "b" the firm should shut down its operations as it cannot cover both variable and total cost.

We can deduce following points from above discussion.

In short run:

If P=>ATC it's the breakeven

AVC<=P<=ATC firm should operate

P<AVC shut down

In long run:

If P=>ATC it's the breakeven

AVC<=P<=ATC shut down

P<AVC shut down

<= means less than or equal to.

Shutdown and break-even point under imperfect competition

The break even and shutdown points can be explained in imperfect competition using MR and MC approach. Remember here we do not have MR =P. We have different curves of MR and AR which are downward sloping (not straight line as in perfect competition).

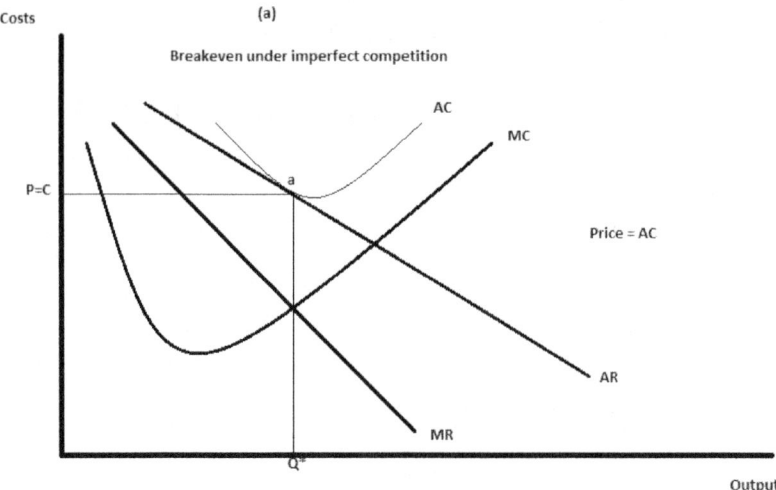

Costs

(a)

Breakeven under imperfect competition

AC

MC

P=C

a

Price = AC

AR

MR

Q*

Output

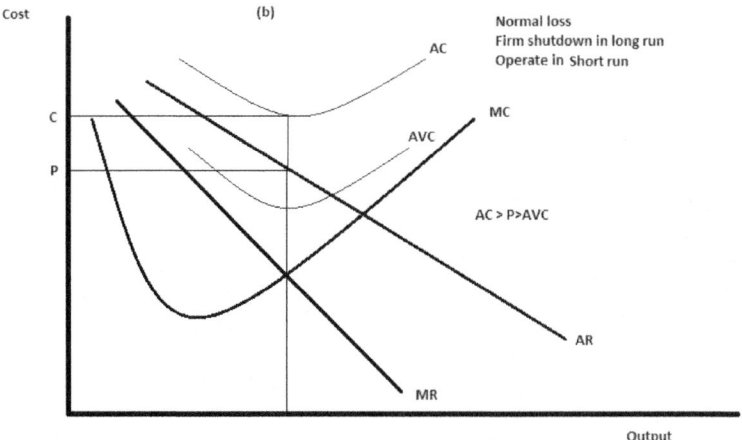

Cost

(b)

AC

Normal loss
Firm shutdown in long run
Operate in Short run

MC

C

AVC

P

AC > P>AVC

AR

MR

Output

As shown in the above figure at point "a" price is equal to AC. At this point the firm is at break even.

If firm is at break even the firm should operate in short run and in long run.

If firm is in (b) figure`s position it should run in short run but should shutdown in long run as price is not covering total average cost but variable cost is being fulfilled.

If even variable cost was not being covered then the firm should shutdown in short and in long run.

LOS 8f: Describe how economies of scale and diseconomies of scale affect costs.

We know that average total cost is U shaped. Long run average total cost curve (LRATC) is made up of joining minimum points of short run average total costs curves. LRATC shows larger scale of production. The minimum point of LRATC is known as minimum efficient scale. The firm should operate at this minimum efficient scale in long run.

In perfect competition the price is equal to the minimum cost and firm earns zero economic profit (also known as normal profit). Production level other than this minimum efficient scale will produce losses.

This LRATC curve decreases at first reaches at lowest point and eventually increases from that lowest point. The decreasing portion of LRATC curve is called **economies of scale** (also known as increasing return to scale).

LRATC decreases due to the factors which are only applicable in large production like labor specialization, massive production, use of more efficient equipments, most sophisticated machinery and plant and also discounts in raw material purchases. This reduction in cost makes the firm more competitive in the market.

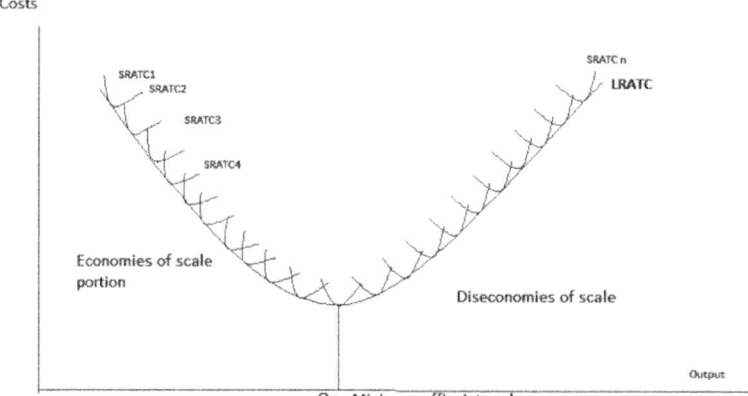

Costs

SRATC1
SRATC2
SRATC3
SRATC4

SRATC n
LRATC

Economies of scale portion

Diseconomies of scale

Output

Qe   Minimum efficeint scale

The area before minimum efficient scale is economies of scale. The area after the minimum efficient scale is diseconomies of scale. At diseconomies of scale marginal cost are increasing while marginal revenues are decreasing. The diseconomies of scale may prevail due to managerial issues (managing larger scale of production may cause inefficiencies), politics involved in big firms, motivation problems with larger workforce.

A firm producing at level above than minimum efficient scale, need to reduce production to achieve Qe.

Points very near to Qe there may be constant return to scale. It means we may have flat LRATC curve there. Constant return to scale means constant costs and constant marginal return in that range.

READING 9: THE FIRM AND MARKET STRUCTURES

We have four major types of market structures. These market structures can be differentiated with respect to following factors.

- Number of firms in the market
- Size of the firm
- Type of elasticity of demand
- Ways and degree of competition
- Ease of entrance into the market

Perfect competition: In this type of market structure large numbers of small firms are producing identical products. New firms are free to enter into the market. There are no barriers for entrance into business. Because of very small size of a firm they have no control over prices. They can sell their entire product at prevailing market prices. So the firms are price taker. And they have perfectly elastic horizontal demand curve. As the products are identical, firms only compete on the basis of prices. Market of agricultural products like wheat, rice can be a good example of perfect competition. The market forces of demand and supply determines the price.

Monopolistic competition: This is the market structure in which many sellers are selling differentiated products. These products are differentiated on the basis of quality, brand name, features or marketing strategies etc. As products are differentiated they are not perfect substitutes. Each firm has elastic (not perfectly elastic) downward demand curve. Also due to differentiated Products a small increase in prices would not make all customers to move away because people are brand conscious. As a result firm has some control over prices of their own product. Firms in this market structure make huge advertisement expenditure for their products to be more attractive. There are some barriers for new firm to enter into the market because the existing firms have occupied their customers who would not move to new products easily.

Oligopoly: This is the market structure where few but large producers are competing with each other. These firms may produce identical or differentiated products. As there are only a few number of firms in the market each firm considers the strategies and responses of other firms in setting their prices, quality and other features of the product. Each firm faces a downward sloping demand curve. Barriers to enter in the market are high. Operating system providers for smart phones, oil and gas Development Industry, auto industry are a good example of oligopoly. Google Android management must consider the Strategies and response of Apple iOS while making their own decisions. The competition in oligopoly market is based on prices brand name or product features.

Monopoly: This is a market structure where only one seller provides the whole supply of a product in the market and there is no close substitute of that product. The firm has full control over price or quantity. If a monopolist wants to sell more he can reduce prices and vice versa. So the firm faces download sloped demand curve. The demand curve of a firm is the demand curve of whole market. The monopolist can threat new firms to enter into the market so the barriers to entrance in the market are very high.

A monopolist exists in the market due to any of the following reasons.

- A monopolist can be protected by copyright or patents.
- Full control over critical resources can also create monopoly.
- Govt. policy can also be a cause of monopoly. In greater public interest govt. creates monopolist. This happens in a situation where average cost of production is lower in some range of production. This is known as

natural monopoly. Public utilities are typical example of natural monopoly.

- Some firms are so deeply penetrated in the markets it becomes almost impossible for other firms to complete with them. This is also a cause of monopoly. Changes in technology and consumer taste can reduce monopoly power.

Following table shows the main characteristics of each market structure.

	Perfect Competition	Monopolistic competition	Oligopoly	Monopoly
Number of sellers	Large	Many	Few	Single
Pricing power	No	Some	Some to significant	Significant
Nature of competition	Price only	Price, huge marketing, Advertisement	Price, huge marketing, Advertise-ment	Not huge advertisement
Substitutes	Very close substitutes	Good substitute but differentiated products	Good substitute Or Differen-tiated products	No substitutes
Barriers to entrance	No	Low	High	Very high

LOS 9b: Explain relationships between price, marginal revenue, marginal cost, economic profit, and the elasticity of demand under each market structure.

LOS 9d: Describe and determine the optimal price and output for firms under each market structure.

LOS 9e: Explain factors affecting long-run equilibrium under each market structure.

We are combining these LOS because they are interrelated and cover whole analyses of all market structures.

Perfect competition: In this type of market structure large numbers of small firms are producing identical products. New firms are free to enter into the market. There are no barriers for entrance into business. Because of very small size of a firm they have no control over prices. They can sell their entire product at prevailing market prices. So the firms are price taker. And they have perfectly elastic horizontal demand curve. As the products are identical firms only compete on the basis of prices. Market of agricultural products like wheat, rice can be a good example of perfect competition. The market forces of demand and supply determines the price.

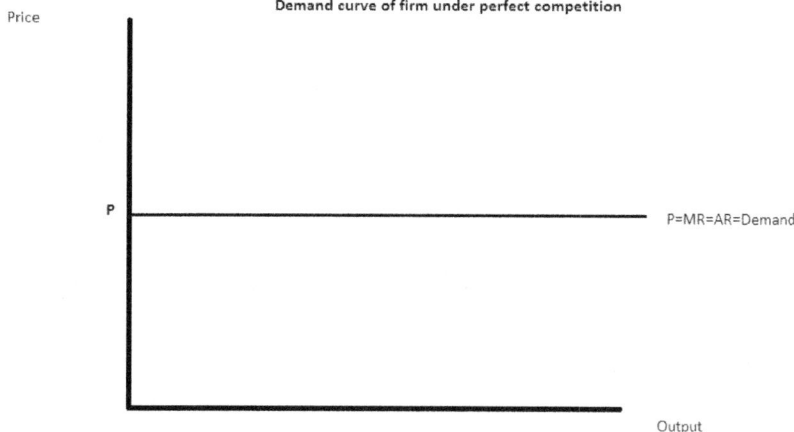

In any market structure a firm should continue its production until its marginal revenue equals marginal cost. The point at which marginal revenues equals marginal cost is called optimal level of production of that firm also known as profit maximizing level of output.

For a firm under perfect competition margin revenues are equal to price because every next unit is sold at same price. That's why a perfectly competitive firm has same marginal revenue, average revenues and demand curve which is perfectly elastic (horizontal line).

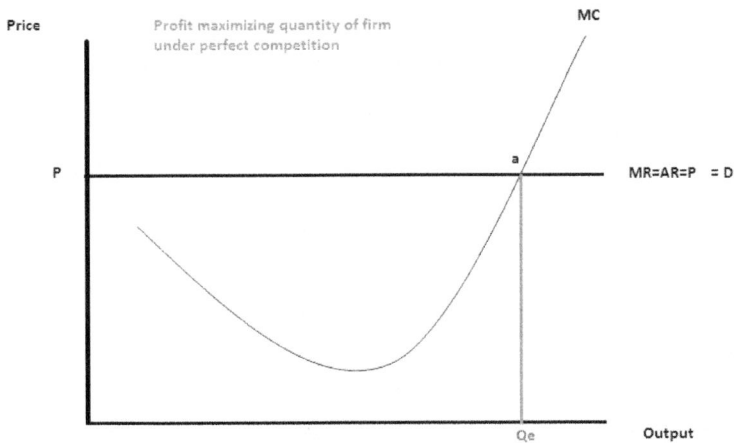

Qe is the profit maximizing quantity of the firm. After the equilibrium we need to see whether the firm in equilibrium is earning profit or in loss. For that we need to add average total cost curve. The rule here is, at equilibrium point if average total cost is below than price the firm is earning economic profit. If average total cost is equal to price the firm is at break even and if average total cost is higher than price the firm is in loss. Let's understand it with the help of graph.

(a)

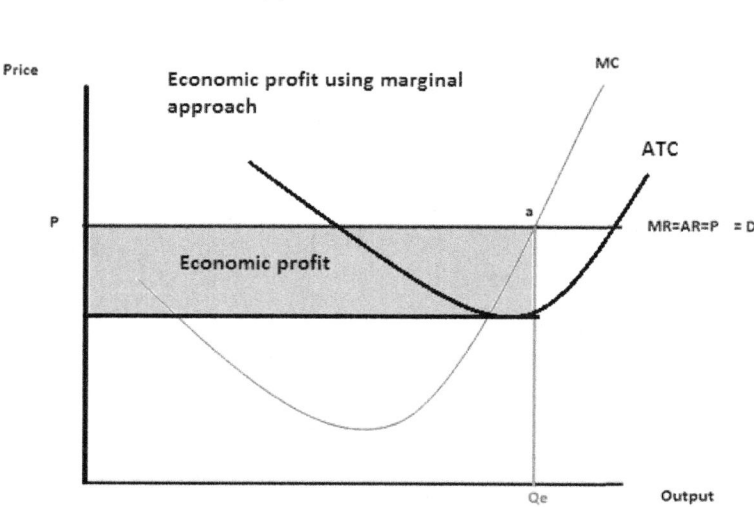

In figure (a) ATC is lower than price at equilibrium the firm is earning economic profit (the shaded area.)

Profit/Accounting profit = Total revenues – Total cost

Economic profit = Total revenues – total cost – opportunity cost.

The firm is earning economic profit in short run. In long run perfectly competitive firm cannot earn economic profit because the new firms enter into the market and share the profits as entry into market is free.

In figure (b) below we used total revenue and total cost approach to show economic profit. In this method the equilibrium point is where the difference between total revenues and total cost is maximum.

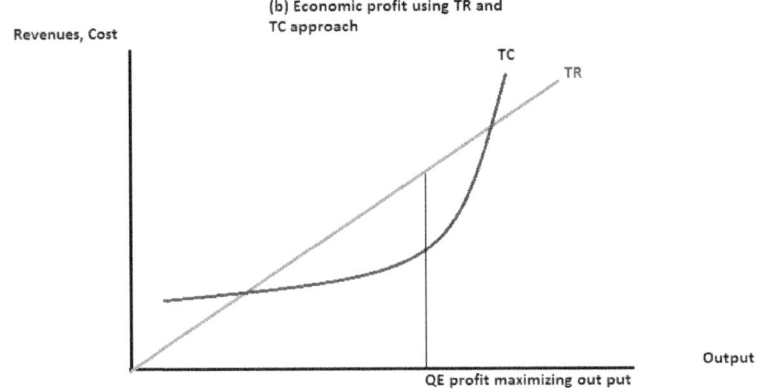

In long run ATC is equal to the price so the firm earns normal profit. With TR and TC approach the equilibrium level of output is the point where difference in total revenues and total cost is at maximum level.

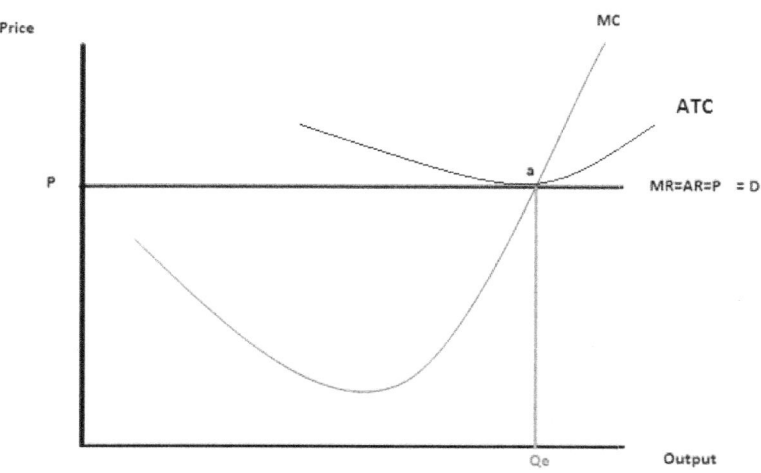

In perfectly competitive market if price is less than average total cost but greater than average variable cost the firm continues its operations in short run. On the other hand if price is so less that it does not cover even average variable cost the firm needs to be shut down even in short run.

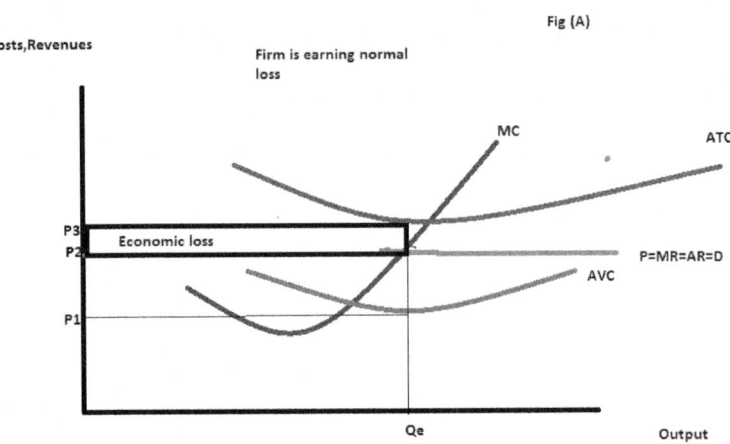

Fig (A)

A perfectly competitive from earns only normal profit in long run because all the firms with losses move out of the market and the firms with only normal profit operates in the market. In long run price is just equal to average total cost. Always remember average total cost includes the opportunity cost so the profits are just enough to keep the firms into the markets.

Under perfect competition the firm operates where p = MC. If the price is below than P1, the firm will shut down. Between P1 and P2 the firm is earning normal loss, so the firm operates in the short run here but not in long run. At the price above than P2 the firm is earning abnormal or economic profit the firm will expand its production along MC. So the short run supply curve of firm is MC curve above average variable cost. The firm will provide more output at higher prices, the supply curve is positively sloped.

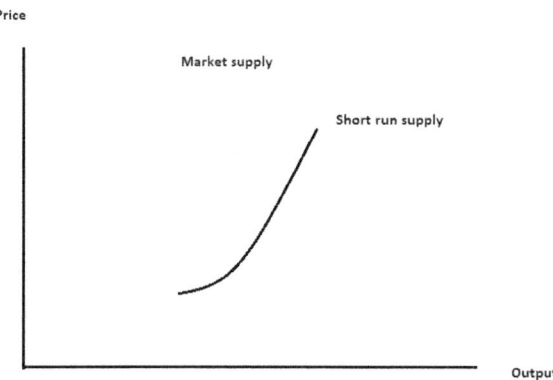

Short run adjustments in the supply and demand under perfect competition

Due to other factors (other than price) the demand can be increased in short run. This increase in demand can shift demand curve upward. On the other hand a decrease in the demand will shift the demand curve downward.

The increase in demand will increase the prices and equilibrium quantity. Decrease in demand will decrease the prices and equilibrium quantity.

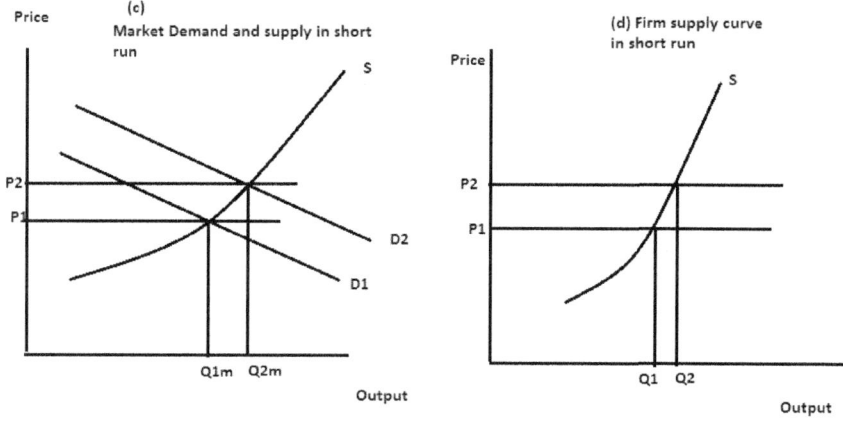

Price

(c)
Market Demand and supply in short run

S

P2

P1

D2

D1

Q1m   Q2m

Output

(d) Firm supply curve in short run

Price

S

P2

P1

Q1   Q2

Output

In p panel (c) we can see that with the increase in the demand from D 1 to D2 will cause an increase in the price from P1 to P2 and equilibrium price and quantity from Q1 to Q2. In panel (d) we can see we increase in the price will leads to higher profits so firms tend to sell more. With this higher price, the firm will be able to earn economic profit in short run. In long run more firms will enter into the markets to share this economic profit. Eventually the market supply will increase and the price will go down.

Downsizing is mostly done to reduce economic losses.

Monopolistic Competition

If the following characteristics exist in the market the market is called monopolistic competition.

1. Large number of independent sellers.
2. Differentiated products are being sold in the market by sellers.
3. The competition is based on price quality and marketing.
3. Barriers to entry of new firms are low.
4. Sellers has some control over the prices of their own product

In monopolistic competition each firm faces downward sloping demand curve. This is mainly because when a firm increases its price the customers have options to move towards other products. That's why there pries elasticity is high.

As we have discussed in perfect competition, a firm in monopolistic competition is in equilibrium or can maximize its profits where marginal revenues are equal to marginal cost (MC=MR).

Output decisions and equilibrium under monopolistic competition

Short run:

In short run monopolistic competitive firm may earn economic profit, normal profit or normal loss.

When average total cost is less than average revenues (price) the firm earns economic profit as shown in the figure below.

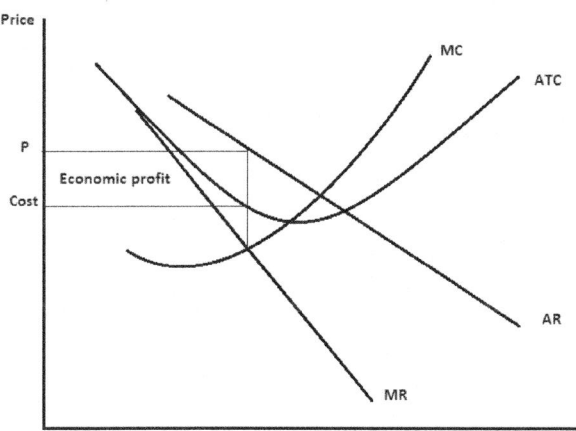

As we have discussed before when average total cost is just equal to price, firm earns normal profits. As shown in the figure below.

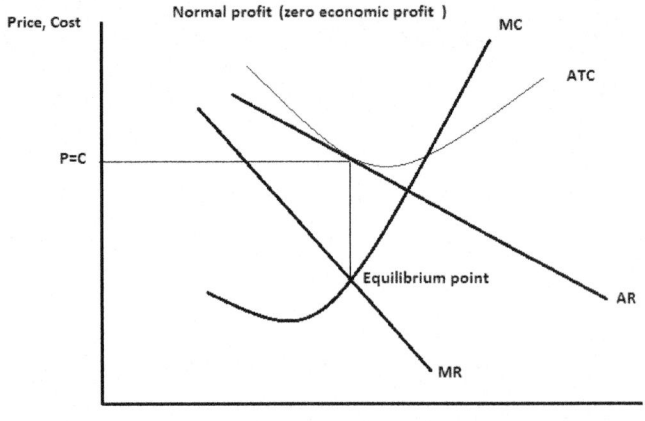

Same way if ATC is higher than price but AVC is below than price it is short run loss for the firm. Firm should continue its production in short run. Firm under monopolistic competition cannot earn abnormal loss because they have some control over price. Even short run normal loss is rare.

Long run: When in short run firm earns economic profit new firms enter into the market and share this profit. So in long run all firms in the market earn normal profit (zero economic profit). Long run equilibrium and output level is shown in following figure.

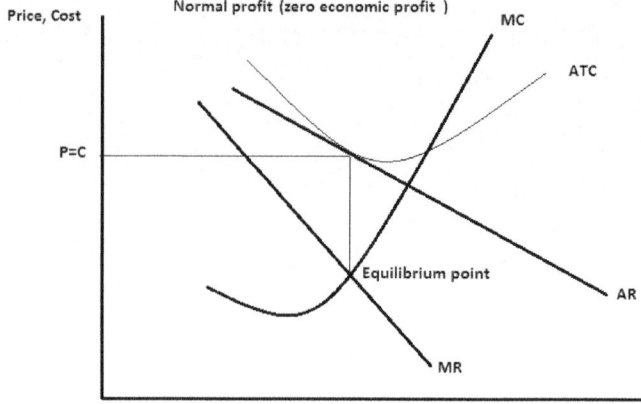

In monopolistic competition the price is always higher than the marginal cost. Another thing to remember here is average total cost is not at its minimum level at equilibrium point. Which means some productive inefficiency or the firm is producing less than its capacity.

Oligopoly

Following are the characteristics of oligopoly market

1. The market is dominated by small number of large firms.

2. The firms either sell differentiated or identical products
3. Barriers to entry are high.

In this market structure all firms are interdependent. It means price changed by one firm will directly affect other firms. Due to complexity of oligopoly market, profit maximizing decisions, demand curve and pricing strategies can be described with the help of following models.

1. Kinked model demand curve model
2. Cournot duopoly model
3. Nash equilibrium (prisoner`s dilemma) model
4. Stackelberg dominant firm model

Kinked model demand curve model

This model has following assumptions

1. The products are close substitutes.
2. The quality of products remains same throughout the analysis and firms do not spend on advertisement.

3. Each firm believes if it reduces the prices the competing firm will follow it but if it increases the prices the other firms will not follow it.
Every firm in the market faces more elastic demand curve (flatter) above a given price and less elastic (steeper) below that given price. (So there is a kink in the demand curve).

We can explain this with the help of following figure.

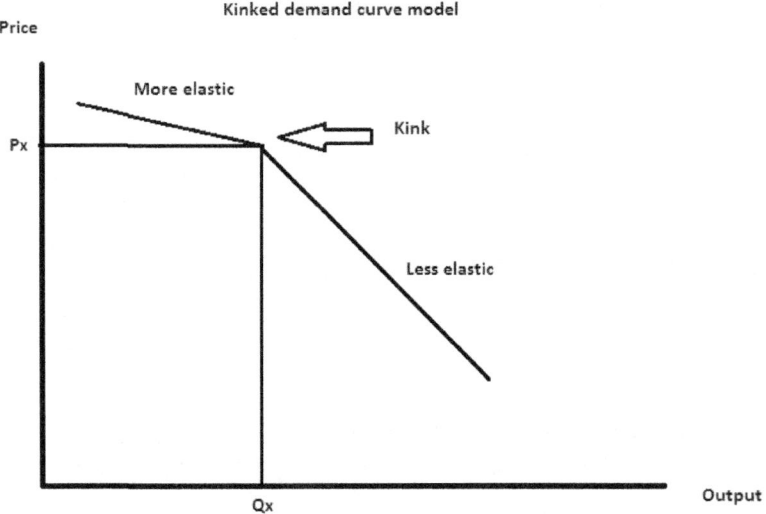

Px is kinked price and Qx is kinked quantity. Above that kinked price the firm faces more elastic demand curve. Therefore moving up from Px will cause the firm to lose the competition as the rival firm will not increase its price

On the other hand if the firm reduces its price from Px the rival firms will also reduce their price, and all the firms will face very little increase in their sales. So the Px is optimal price/ profit maximizing level and Qx is profit maximizing or optimal level of output.

Marginal revenues under kinked demand model

The MR curve is in discontinuous shape under this model.

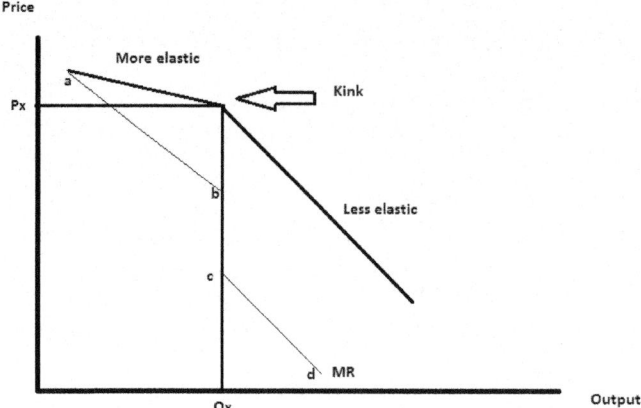

The MR curve is in discontinuous shape. The *ab* part of MR is related to more elastic demand curve while *cd* part of MR is linked to less elastic demand curve.

The equilibrium is where MC intersects MR as following

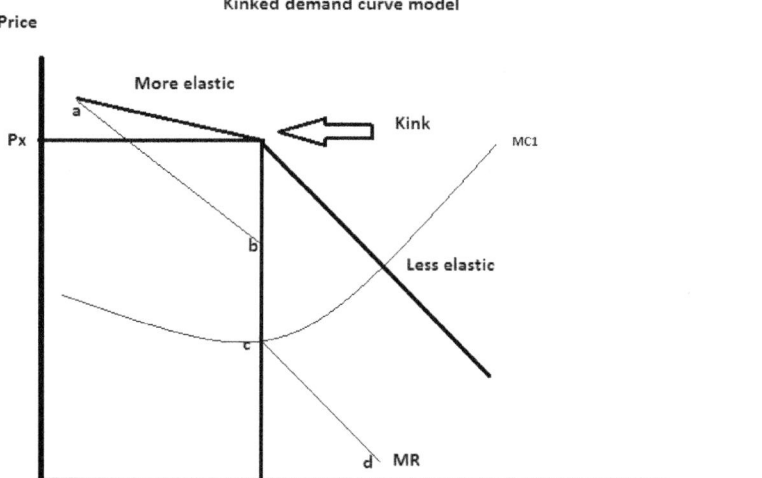

Kinked demand curve model

MC intersects the MR at point c. So the equilibrium point of output is Qx. Now if the cost increases marginal cost curve will move upward to MC 2. In this case the firm cannot increase its price because other firms will not increase their prices and our firm will lose its customers. Moreover the profits will remain same between the points *b* and *c*, so there is no motivation to increase the price. Therefore price and output will remain the same.

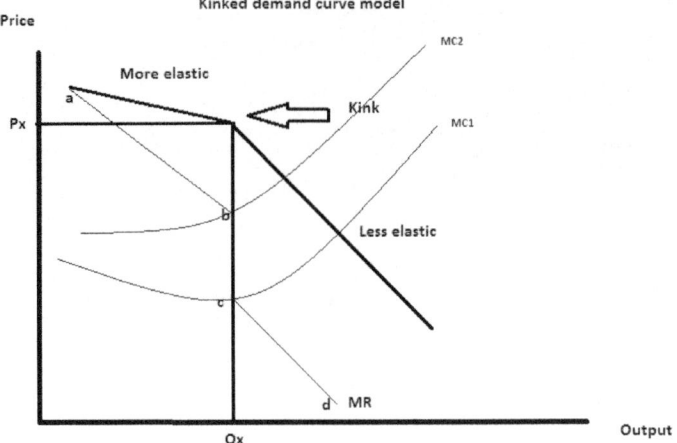

Kinked demand curve model

Criticism on kinked model

This model is criticized by many economists on following grounds.

1. This model only emphasizes on price rigidity but does not explain determination of price.
2. The assumption of upward rigidity of prices is not true.
3. It ignores non price competitions like product differentiation, advertisement etc.
4. Model ignored price leadership and cartels effects.

5.

Cournot duopoly model

It was developed by "A. Cournot" in 1838. Following are the assumptions of this model

1. There are two firms competing in the market (duopoly).
2. Both firms have identical and constant marginal cost curves.
3. Each firm knows the quantity of output provided by the other firm in previous period and assume that it will supply the same in next period. By subtracting that quality from the market demand the firm can construct its own marginal revenue and demand curve and also can determine its own profit maximizing level of output.

Each firm determines its quantity of output simultaneously until both firms have equal quantity. This quantity is optimal quantity of output. This means no one can gain from change in its quantity of output. This also means at these qualities we have stable equilibrium. Equilibrium price is lower than monopolist but higher than perfect competition. This price is also higher than marginal cost of the firms in duopoly. If more firms are added into this model the price gets lower and eventually becomes equal to marginal cost.

Cournot model is considered as the initial version of strategic game. Strategic game means the model in which best choices of one firm depends on the actions of other firms.

A better version of strategic game model is developed by john Nash, called Nash equilibrium.

5. Nash equilibrium (prisoner`s dilemma) model

John Nash developed this model. Nash equilibrium is obtained when no participant (firm) can gain (increase profit or decrease loss) by changing his own strategy when strategies of other participants (firms) are unchanged.

Prisoner`s dilemma is a standard example of Nash equilibrium in game theory. Two prisoners, prisoner 1 and prisoner 2, are believed to commit a serious crime. However it is very hard for prosecutor to prove the crime. So the prisoners are separated and offered following deal.

If Prisoner 1 confesses and Prisoner 2 remains quiet, Prisoner 1 goes free and Prisoner 2 receives an 8 year sentence.
If Prisoner 2 confesses and Prisoner 1 remains quiet, Prisoner 2 goes free and Prisoner 1 receives an 8 year sentence.
If both prisoners remain quiet, each will receive a 6-month sentence.
If both prisoners confess, each will receive a 2-year sentence.

Each prisoner can either betray other by confessing or coordinate by remaining silent. But no one knows what other is going to choose.

Following table shows the result of each outcome

	Prisoner 2 is quiet	Prisoner 2 confess
Prisoner1 is quiet	Prisoner 1 gets 6 months Prisoner 2 gets 6 months	Prisoner 1 gets 8 years Prisoner 2 goes free
Prisoner 1 confess	Prisoner 1 goes free Prisoner 2 gets 8 years punishment	Prisoner 1 gets 2 years Prisoner 2 gets 2 years punishment

It is clear from table that the best overall outcome for both prisoners is to remain quiet and get 6 month sentence. But this is not Nash equilibrium because each Prisoner can improve his situation from quiet/quiet by confessing. A quiet Prisoner can improve its situation by confessing and going free. Confess/confess is the **Nash equilibrium**, because in this situation no one can improve its position by changing the strategy.

Another and easy way to view this is that, no matter what other Prisoner is going to do the best strategy for each prisoner is to confess.

We can use this prisoner`s dilemma game for duopoly. As in prisoner`s dilemma Nash equilibrium is where both prisoners confess, in following example it's for both firms to cheat on each other. They agreed on a deal of collusive cooperation and charging high price. But each can earn extra profit by cheating.

	Firm B cooperate	Firm B cheats
Firm A Cooperate	A earns economic profit B earns economic profit	A earns loss B earns extra economic profit
Firm B cheats	A earns extra economic profit B earns loss	A earns normal (zero economic) profit B earns normal (zero economic) profit

Nash equilibrium is where both firms cheats and earn zero economic profit. Although the best strategy for each firm is to cooperate and honor the deal of charging high price. But each firm can improve its situation by cheating. If both cheat no firm can improve its situation by changing its own strategy.

LIBOR fixation, oil price fixations are some examples of collusive agreements but we saw that some firms occasionally cheated to obtain optimal profits. This cheating also comes from anti-trust laws by which govt. discourage cartels.

In collusive agreement to increase the prices and fewer tendencies to cheat happens when there are fewer firms in the market, producing similar products (more similar less cheating), and firms have similar cost structures, less competition from outside of cartel and severe retaliation from other firms if anyone cheats.

6. Stackelberg dominant firm model

In this model of oligopoly, there is a single dominant firm. The firm is dominant because of it lower cost structure and higher market share. This dominant firm set the price while other firms in the market follow this price. So the dominant firm is price setter and follower firms are price taker.

The dominant firm set the price according to its MC. Other firms have higher cost curves than dominant firms. They usually cannot charge lower price. If they do in short run the dominant firm can reduce its own price and other firms may be kicked out of the business because they will bear losses. In a result dominant firm believes the quantity supplied by other smaller firms will fall as price falls so the demand curve of dominant firm (DF) is related to the market demand as follows.

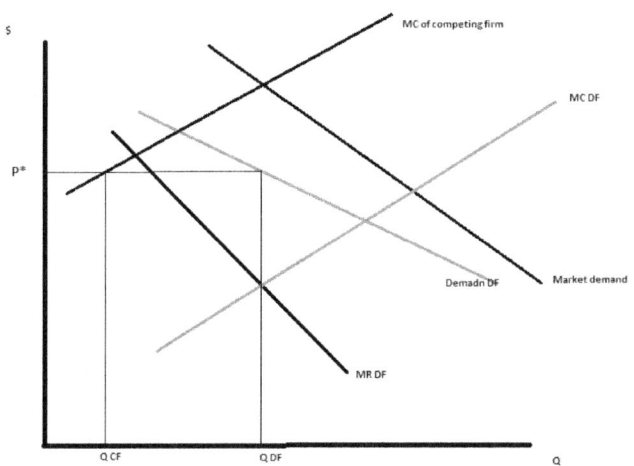

This is dominant firm (DF) oligopoly model. The DF will optimize its own profit at Q DF and P*. The competing firm will optimize its profit by producing quantity (QCF) equal to its MC.

Monopoly

This is exactly opposite to perfect competition. When there is single firm in the market providing whole market supply and there is no close substitution of that product in market the market structure is called monopoly. The barriers to entry of new firm are very high so the firm earns economic profit especially in long run. A monopolist firm has full control over its price or quantity. It means if the firm wants to sale more it must reduce its price and vice versa. The monopolist firm must determine optimal price for its product to get maximum profit. So the monopolist faces downward sloped demand curve.

A monopolist can adopt two types of pricing strategies, Single price and price discrimination.

In single pricing strategy firm charge one price in all markets and from all types of customers. This price is charged when price discrimination is not possible. Price discrimination means charging different prices to different types of customers and or charging different price in different markets. Price discrimination is only effective when customers cannot resell the purchased products.

Profit maximization:

A monopolist firm (like other market structures) maximizes its profit where its MR equals MC.

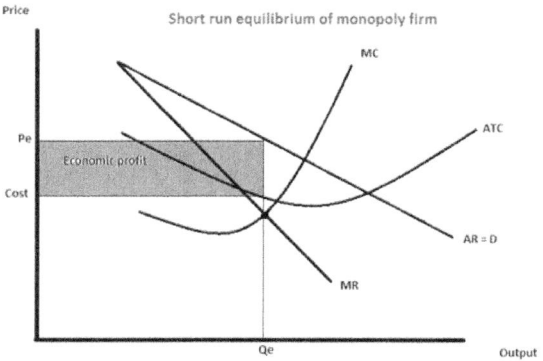

From the figure above we can see that monopoly equilibrium occurs where MC =

MR. for equilibrium price we go to AR from equilibrium point. We come up with Pe the equilibrium price. By going down we get the equilibrium quantity Qe. The difference between equilibrium price and cost is profit.

We know that; profit = TC – TR = TC – (PxQ).

Monopoly equilibrium/profit maximization using price discrimination strategy:

Price discrimination means charging different prices to different types of customers and or charging different prices in different markets. Age discounts, occupational discounts, gender based pricing are some examples of price discrimination.

Following are some prerequisites for price discrimination.

1. The seller must face downward sloping demand curve.

2. The seller must have at least two identifiable groups of customers with different elasticity of demand.
3. The seller must be able to prevent the re-selling of his product.

A monopolist can increase its profit by charging discriminated price. The following figure shows how price discrimination can increase the total quantity and profits of the firm in comparison to single price strategy. For simplicity we assumed no fixed cost and constant variable cost. So, our MC and ATC are same.

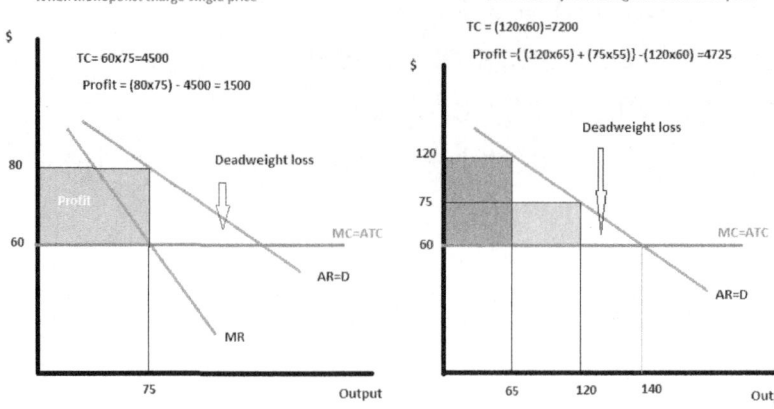

When monopolist charge single price, he sold 75 units at 80$ per unit. His total cost is 60x75 = 4500$. TR are 80x75 = 6000$. So the profit is 1500$.

On the other hand when he charged discriminated price his total profit increases as initially he sold 65 units at $120 per unit. Additionally he sold further 55 units at $75/unit. So his total revenues in this case are (120x65) + (75x55) =7800 + 4125 = 11925

Cost is 120 x 60 = 7200. Profit would be 11925- 7200 = 4725

It is clear from above figures that monopolist get more profit when he charge the discriminated price.

Monopoly is considered to be less efficient than perfect competition because it reduces consumer and producers surplus known as dead weight loss shown in the figures. If you look carefully the deadweight loss is higher in single price and lower in discriminated price. Because in case of discriminated price consumer who are willing to pay high are charged high. That's why in discriminated price monopolist increase its surplus by taking away the consumer surplus.

If our monopolist is able to charge each customer a maximum price they want to pay the dead weight loss can be completely eliminated. This phenomenon is called perfect price discrimination and is mostly considered as theoretical.

Natural monopoly: Sometimes in the market the startup cost of doing business is very high or the fixed cost of doing business is very high. In this case natural monopolist exists in the market. It is beneficial for general public to have single firm in the market. Sometimes natural monopoly exists because the raw material or technology required for business is very unique.

The average cost of production of single firm decreases with more production. For example, an electricity supplying company. Cost of building power lines and other equipment required huge capital. But the marginal cost of providing additional electricity is very low.

So we can say that when average cost of producing extra unit is getting lower and lower a natural monopoly exist in the market.

If we allow a new firm to enter into the market the average cost of both firms will be high, in this case consumers will get higher prices.

As monopolist tend to produce less than their optimal level of quantity to get highest profits at higher prices government tries to regularize natural monopolies in the following ways.

Average cost pricing: This is the most common way of regularization. By doing this government forces the monopolist to reduce the prices to the level where average total cost is equal to market demand. This would increase the production and decrease the prices and reduces the profit.

Marginal cost pricing: With this strategy government forces the monopolist to reduce the price at a level where marginal cost equal to the demand. This is called efficient regulation. In such case if the firm bears some losses, the government needs to provide subsidy so the firm would not leave the market.

LOS 9c: Describe a firm's supply function under each market structure.

Under Perfect competition: Under perfect competition short run supply curve is the marginal cost curve about its average variable cost curve as we have described in previous L O S.

The market supply curve is simply, sum of all firms` individual supply curves.

Under Monopoly oligopoly and monopolistic competition: In Monopoly oligopoly and monopolistic competition there is no well defined supply function. The quantity supplied under these market structures depends upon firm`s marginal cost, its demand and on its marginal revenues. In these market structures all firms face downward sloping demand curves. The quantities supplied are determined by the marginal cost and marginal revenue`s intersection while the price is determined by the demand curve of the firm. In perfect competition the price was equal to marginal revenue but here this is not the case.

We have discussed this in previous section, here we make a quick summary.

Perfect competition: Under perfect competition a firm maximizes its profit by producing the quantity at which marginal cost is equal to marginal revenues (MC=MR). We know that under perfect competition marginal revenue and price is same. So MC=MR=P=D at profit maximization level.

Monopolistic competition: Under monopolistic competition profits are maximized by producing the quantity where marginal revenues are equal to marginal cost same as in another market structures. Firm operating under monopolistic competition faces downward sloping demand curve. Price would be higher than the marginal cost and marginal revenue.

Monopoly: Same as monopolistic competition firm operating under Monopoly can maximize its profit by producing the quantity where marginal avenues are equal to marginal cost. Also like monopolistic competition the firm faces is downward sloping demand curve and the price is greater than marginal revenues and marginal cost.

Oligopoly: Under oligopoly the pricing and output decisions are interdependent on the decisions of other firms, the optimal pricing strategy will depend on what model we are considering.

1. *Kinked demand curve model:* Under this model if a firm reduces its prices the competitive firm will also reduce its price but if a firm increase its price the competitive firm will not increase his price. Here the firm maximizes its profit by producing a quantity where its marginal cost is equal to marginal revenues. The marginal revenue curve is discontinuous with kinked demand curve. In the discontinuous area the firm can produce its optimal level of output.
2. *Cournot duopoly model:* Each firm determinants its quantity of output in simultaneously until both firms have equal quantity. This quantity is optimal quality of

output. This means no one can gain from change in its quantity of output. This also means at these qualities we have stable equilibrium. Equilibrium price is lower than monopolist but higher than perfect competition. This price is also higher than marginal cost of the firms in duopoly. If more firms are added into this model the price gets lower and eventually becomes equal to marginal cost.

3. ***Nash equilibrium (prisoner`s dilemma) model:*** Nash equilibrium is where both firms cheats and earn zero economic profit. Although the best strategy for each firm is to cooperate and honor the deal of charging high price. But each firm can improve its situation by cheating. If both cheat no firm can improve its situation by changing its own strategy.

4. ***Stackelberg dominant firm model:*** In this model of oligopoly, there is single dominant firm. This dominant firm set the price while other firms in the market follow this price. So the dominant firm is price setter and follower firms are price taker. The dominant firm set the price according to its MC. Other firms have higher cost curves than dominant firms. They usually cannot charge lower price. If

they do in short run the dominant firm can reduce its own price and other firms may be kicked out of the business because they will bear losses. In a result dominant firm believes the quantity supplied by other smaller firms will fall as price falls so the demand curve of dominant firm (DF) is related to the market demand

LOS 9g: Describe the use and limitations of concentration measures in identifying market structure.

Different measures are used to examine the pricing power of a firm in an industry.

These measures include elasticity of demand, percentage of market sales, and concentration measures. These measures are used to determine degree of monopoly/market power of a firm in the industry. Concentration measures are easier than elasticity measures. One most commonly used concentration measure is N-firm concentration ratio. Larger the concentration ratio less the competition is. This is calculated by summing percentage share of largest "n" firms in an industry. For example firm A has total sale to market sales (firm`s sales/market sales) of 20%. Firm B has 15%, firm C has 12%. N-firm concentration is calculated as 20+15 +12=37%.

This is very simple measure to calculate and understand but it also has drawbacks. It does not measure elasticity and market power directly. It also does not cover the mergers of different firms. This problem is eliminated by using alternative concentration ratio which is **Herfindahl-Hirschman Index** (HHI). This is calculated by sum of squares of market percentages of top n firms.

By using previous example we can calculate HHI as follows

$20^2 + 15^2 + 12^2 = 769$

The concentration measures also don't consider the barriers of entrance into the market. A firm might have huge market share but if market has lower barriers to enter into the market, the firm may not have the high pricing or market power.

LOS 9h: Identify the type of market structure within which a firm operates.

We can identify the market structure within which a firm operates by using following characteristics

1. Number of firms in the industry
2. Nature of barriers to entry
3. Nature of substitutes available
4. Nature of competition
5. Pricing power of firm

We can understand this with the help of following table

	Perfect competition	Monopolistic competition	Oligopoly	Monopoly
Number of firms	Large number	Many firms	Few firms	Single firm

Nature of barriers	Free entry	Low barriers	High barriers	Very high barriers
Nature of substitutes available	Perfect or very good substitutes	Good substitutes but differentiated products	Close substitutes or differentiated products	No close substitute
Nature of competition	Only price	Price, marketing and features of products	Price, marketing and features of products	Low advertisement
Pricing power of firm	No power	Some power	me to significant	Significant power

READING 10: AGGREGATE OUTPUT, PRICES, AND ECONOMIC GROWTH

LOS 10a: Calculate and explain gross domestic product (GDP) using expenditure and income approaches.

Gross domestic product (GDP): Market value of all final goods and services produced within boundaries of a country in one year is called gross domestic product.

Market value means the price at which the goods or services are being sold in the market.

Final goods means the price of computer chips are not included but the price of final product of computers/laptops is included. Some goods are intermediate goods. These are the goods which are under process and they are not ready to be used by final customer. They need to be processed further and must not be included in the calculation of GDP.

Within boundaries means those goods and services are included in the GDP which are produced within a country. Anything produced outside of country even by nationals of a country are not included in GDP of that country. On the other hand if a foreigner is producing goods or services in a country that will be included in the GDP of that country.

We also do not include the goods being resold. Only those goods and services are included which are produced within the current year.

Goods and services produced by governments are also included in the GDP at their cost because they are not being sold in the market so their market value cannot be determined.

Calculation of GDP

We have 4 factors of production be used to produce goods and services. These factors are land, labor, capital and Organization. The reward for land is rent for capital it is interest, for labor we pay wages and for the organization the reward is profit. These rents wages interest and profits are income of the households and businesses. Sum of all these is GDP by **income approach**.

Under expenditure approach we add all the expenditures on production of goods and services during that period (one year).
The GDP must be the same using either method.

LOS 10b: Compare the sum-of-value-added and value-of-final-output methods of calculating GDP.

Value-of-final-output methods: We can add the value of all final goods and services in GDP calculation, the method is called value of final output method. The expenditure approach is also called value of final output method.

Sum of value added method: In this method we simply add the value added at each stage of the production. For example when wheat is produced we add the market value of that wheat. When it is purchased by a baker and he produce the loaves of bread, we do not add the market value of bread but the additions in market value made by the Baker is added into the value of wheat.

Again we must come up with the same GDP by using any approach.

LOS 10c: Compare nominal and real GDP and calculate and interpret the GDP deflator.

We know that GDP is the market value of all final goods and services produced within the country in one year. If GDP is calculated by using current market prices we have **nominal GDP**. For a country with N different goods and services we calculate the nominal GDP as

$$\text{Nominal GDP for the year } t = \sum_{i=1}^{N} (P_{i,t} \times Q_{i,t})$$

$P_{i,t}$ is the price of good/ service i in year t.
$Q_{i,t}$ is quantity of good/ service i produced in year t.

Nominal GDP is affected by the increasing prices even without any increase in quantity of goods and services.

Real GDP: When we calculate GDP by using base year prices we come up with real GDP. Real GDP eliminates the effect of increase in prices. So it is unaffected by inflation and we get some better result of economic growth. Base year means some previous year with certain qualities like stability in prices.
We calculate real GDP for N number of goods and services as follows

$$\text{Nominal GDP for the year } t = \sum_{i=1}^{N} (P_{i,tb} \times Q_{i,t})$$

Where P(tb) means prices at base year.

GDP deflator: GDP deflator is a metric used to eliminate the effect of inflation on nominal GDP.
GDP deflator can be calculated as

$$\text{GDP deflator} = \frac{Nominal\ GDP}{Real\ GDP}\ x\ 100$$

With the help of GDP deflator we can convert nominal GDP into real GDP as follows,

$$Real\ GDP = \frac{Nominal\ GDP}{GDP\ deflator}\ x\ 100$$

LOS 10d: Compare GDP, national income, personal income, and personal disposable income.

We know that GDP is the market value of all final goods and services produced within the country in one year. We do not include the income from the factors abroad in GDP.

National Income: It is the total value of all services goods and services produced within the country and the income from abroad. We also deduct the incomes of foreign factors working in our country.

National income is simply the income received by all factors of production of our country in one year.

National income includes employee`s wages and benefits, private and government Enterprises profits before taxes, interest income, rent, indirect business taxes less subsidies.

So the national income = GDP + income from abroad - income of foreign factors in our country – capital consumption allowance.

Capital consumption allowance: Capital consumption allowance is the amount of money a country has to spend to main its present level of economic production. These are the expenditures on capital goods.

Personal income (PI): It is total a pre-tax income received by the households.

Personal income = *national income + transfer payments to households – indirect business taxes – corporate income taxes – undistributed corporate profits.*

Personal disposable income (PDI): The personal income after taxes is called personal disposable income it is the actual processing power of the households.

Personal disposable income = personal income – personal taxes

LOS 10e: Explain the fundamental relationship among saving, investment, the fiscal balance, and the trade balance.

In calculation of GDP using expenditure approach, the following are the components of GDP.

GDP = C + I + G + (X-M)

C

C = conception expenditures

I= investment

G = government expenditures

X-M= net Exports

X= exports

M= imports

While using income method the GDP must be calculated as

GDP= C + S + T

As using both methods we must have same GDP these two equations can be equal

C + I + G + (X-M) = C + S + T

When we solve this equation for S we get following relationship

$$S = I + (G - T) + (X - M)$$

G - T is the physical balance. A positive G - T means fiscal deficit as government expenditures are more than tax collection. A negative (G - T) means fiscal surplus.

The above equation shows savings must be equal to private investment + government borrowings or minus government savings - trade deficits or plus trade surplus.

If we solve the equation for fiscal balance we get

$$(G - T) = (S - I) - (X - M)$$

This equation shows the government deficit must be financed by the trade deficit and or private savings minus Investments.

Los 10f: Explain how the aggregate demand curve is generated.

We know that

$$GDP = C + I + G + (X-M)$$

Let's understand all these factors in detail first.

Consumption: Consumption depends on disposable income. So the consumption is a function of disposable income. Increase in disposable income will increase the consumption while a decrease in the taxes will also increase the consumption and other way around. This disposable income is either consumed or saved. Proportion of additional unit of income which is consumed is called marginal propensity to consume (MPC) and the proportion which is saved is called marginal propensity to save.
MPS + MPC =100% {Means 100% of total income}

{MPC = ΔC/ ΔY, where ΔC is change in consumption and ΔY is change in income. MPS = Δ S/ Δ Y where Δ S is change in savings}

Investment: Investment is a function of expected profitability and the cost of financing (also called interest rate). The profitability depends upon the output. And interest rate is real interest rate which is nominal interest rate minus expected inflation rate.

Government spending depends on the tax revenues of the Government and tax revenues depends upon the output produced by the economy so the government expenditures depends upon the output in the economy.

Net exports are function of domestic disposable income and foreign disposable income. Domestic disposable income affects the imports and foreign disposable income affects the exports of our country.

IS curve is income saving curve. It shows the negative relationship between real interest rate and real income for the equilibrium in goods market. All points on IS curve shows the different combinations of real interest rate and real output (income) on which there is an equilibrium in goods market.

Real interest rate

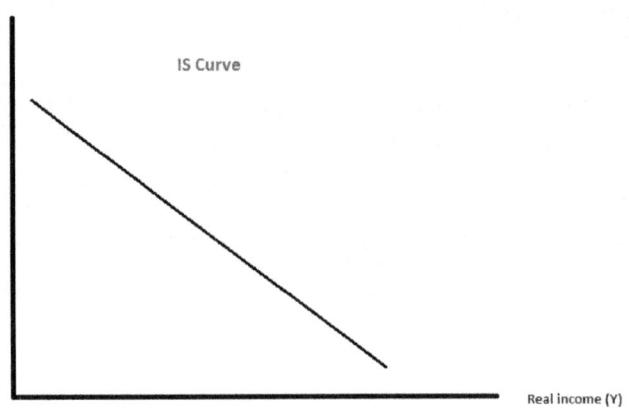

IS Curve

Real income (Y)

This happens due to following channel. With the decrease in interest rate, people save less and consume more. The demand for goods and services increases. So the investors will produce more products and services. The investment also increases due to low cost of borrowing (i.e. low interest rate). The net effect of a reduction in interest rate is increase in the investment and aggregate demand. This is the reason I S curve is negatively sloped between interest rate and output.

LM curve: It is liquidity preference- money supply curve. It gives us all the combinations of income and real interest rate for which money market is in equilibrium (demand for real money = real supply of money). It is positively sloped curve.

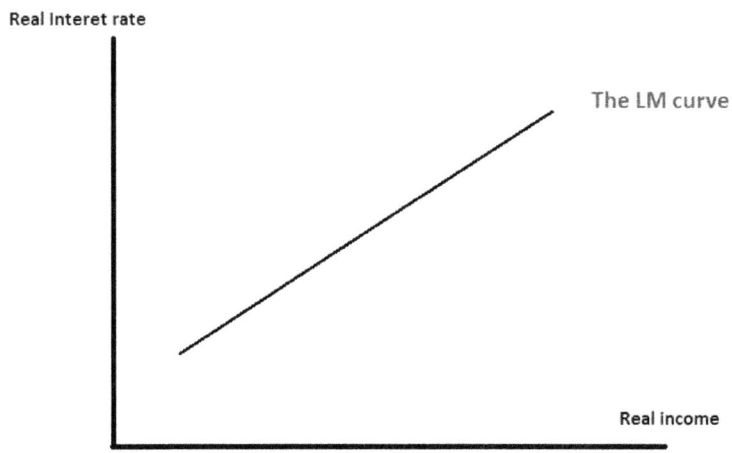

Real Interet rate

The LM curve

Real income

The shortest channel of deriving LM curve is, when real income rises, the demand for money increases. Rise in demand for money increases the real interest rate to equilibrate the supply of money. The net effect is positive relationship between real income and real interest rate.

The equilibrium in both goods and money market exists where both IS and LM curves interest with each other.

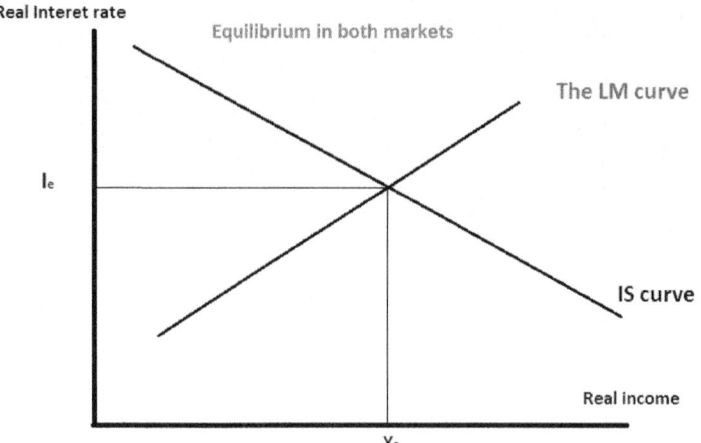

Here 'Ie' is the equilibrium real interest rate while 'Ye' is equilibrium real output level.

Aggregate demand curve

AD curve shows the negative relationship between demand for output and price level. It is a total quantity of goods and services demanded in an economy at different price level.

Derivation of aggregate demand curve

In derivation of LM curve we held the real money supply (M/P) constant. Increase in the price level will decrease the real money supply (M/P). That will shift the LM curve upward. A decrease in price level will increase the real money supply so it will make LM curve to shift downward. The upward and downward shift of the LM curve is shown in the following figure.

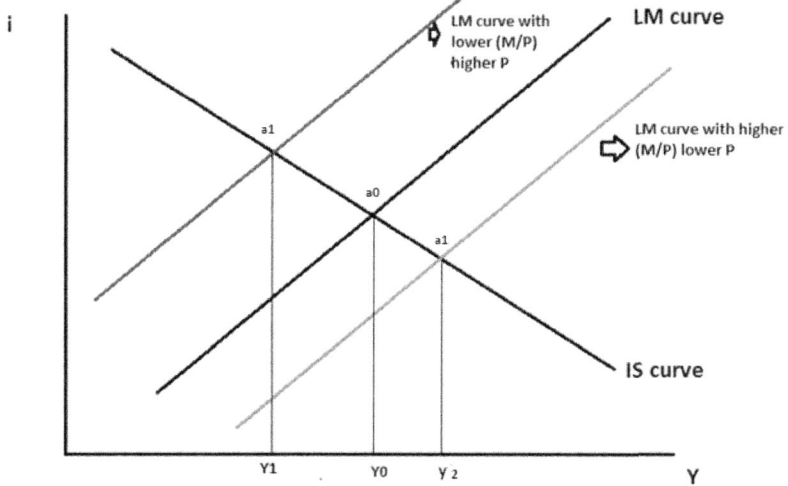

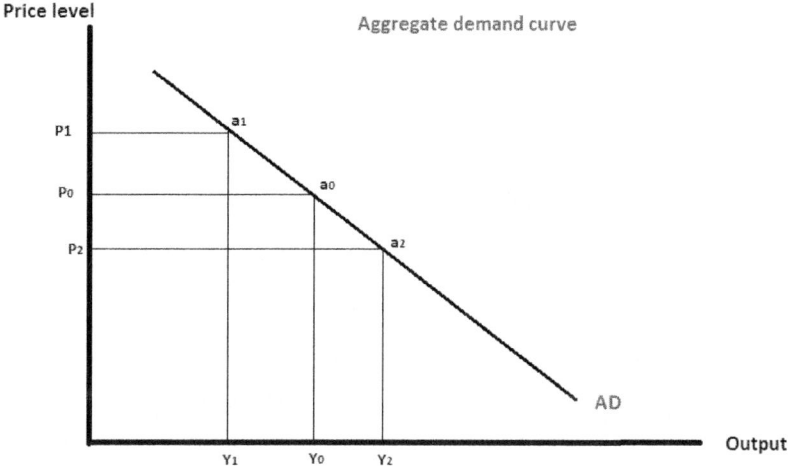

Keeping real money supply constant we have downward sloping aggregate demand curve, because higher price level reduce the demand and low price level increases the demand. High price level also reduces the real wealth of the consumers so the purchasing power also decreases that's another reason for downward sloping demand curve.

LOS 10g: Explain the aggregate supply curve in the short run and long run.

Keeping other thing constant AS curve shows the positive relationship between real GDP and price level. We have three types of aggregate supply curve with respect to time.

1. **Very short run AS curve:** In very short run all costs are fixed. Firms only adjust their output by changing the labor hours and intensity of plant use. Firms do not change their prices in VSRAS. SRAS curve is perfectly elastic.

2. **Short run AS curve:** In short run aggregate supply curve, prices of some factors of production are fixed and some are variables. Aggregate output is highly sensitive to the price level. Some inputs prices increases but firms do not perceive it as increase in input prices but they see it

as increase in profits so they increase their output. So in short run aggregate supply curve is positively sloped.

3. **Long run AS curve:** LRAS curve is perfectly inelastic. All costs are variable in long run. All input prices changes proportionately to the increase in prices. The firms have no motivation to increase their output. So in long run price level has no effect on AS. We call it <u>full employment GDP or potential GDP</u>.

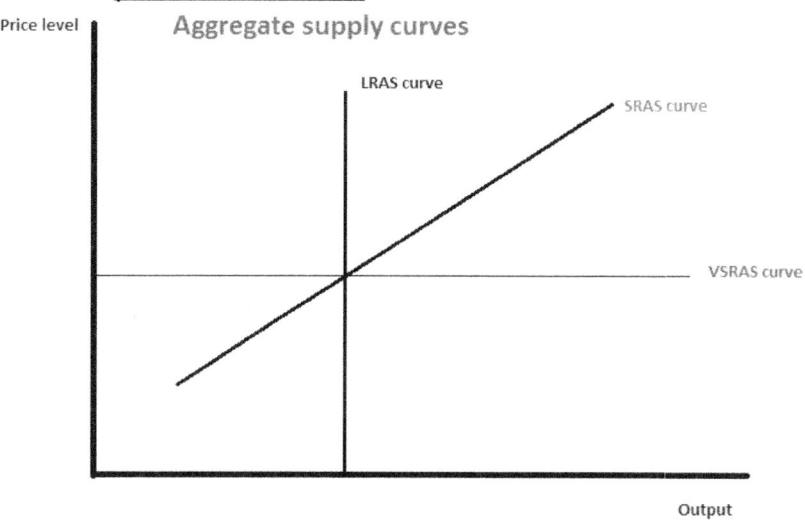

LOS 10h: Explain causes of movements along and shifts in aggregate demand and supply curves.

Movement along Aggregate Demand and Supply Curves

Movement along both AS and AD curves are due to change in price level. When price level increases the aggregate demand will decrease while increase in price level will increase aggregate supply and vice versa. The changes in price level do not shift either of the curves.

Shift in AD curve:

Aggregate demand is the total demand of goods and services by consumers, businesses, government and foreigners. So
AD = C + I + G + NX
Any increase or decrease in any of these factors will shift the aggregate demand curve forward or backward. If consumers increase their demand for goods and services that mean C is increasing. This will shift the demand curve forward or upward. Same is the case with I, G and NX.
Factors which shift the aggregate demand,
1. Increase in consumer`s wealth: When the wealth of consumers like real estate, stocks etc. increases they demand more and

more goods/services. The result would be upward shift in the aggregate demand curve. On the other hand if consumer's wealth decreases aggregate demand will shift backward or downward.

2. Business expectations: When the people involved in businesses expect high profitability in future they tend to demand more investment goods. That will shift the aggregate demand curve forward.

3. Expansionary monetary policy: Expansionary monetary policy means central Bank increases the money supply and reduces the interest rate. The banks will have more funds to lend. People will have more money in their hands or in their accounts. They want more goods and services. It will shift the aggregate demand curve forward. When the interest rate is reduced businesses takes the opportunity and borrow this money and use it to install more plants and machinery. So, the investment expenditures will increase. That will shift aggregate demand curve forward.

4. **Expansionary fiscal policy:** Expansionary fiscal policy means reduction in the taxes and or increase in the government spending. Reduction in taxes will increase the disposable personal income so the

consumption increases while the government expenditures increases AD directly. These both effects will increase the aggregate demand and shift the aggregate demand curve forward.

5. **World economic growth:** Economic growth in other countries will also shift the aggregate demand curve forward. When a country grows it imports more goods and services. So the economic growth in other countries will shift our AD curve forward.

6. **Consumer`s expectations:** If households expect an increase in the wages, they tend to spend more. It shifts the aggregate demand curve forward.

7. **Currency devaluation:** Devaluation of domestic currency will make the imports costly for residents of our country while the exports will increase. As our products would become cheaper for foreigners, aggregate demand curve will shift forward.

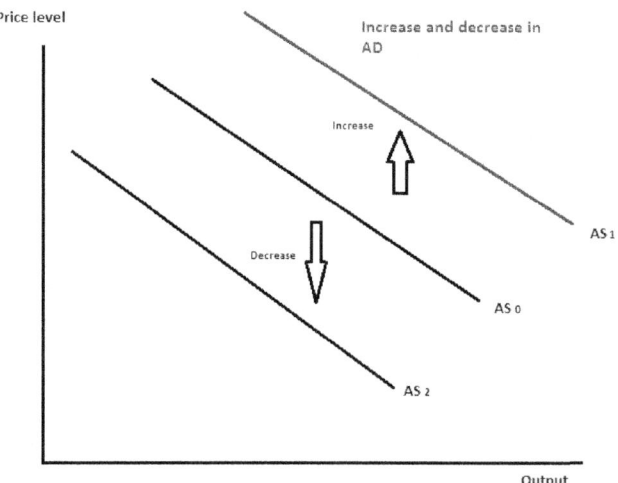

Shift in Aggregate supply curve

Shift in aggregate supply curve can be seen in two ways
1. Shift in AS curve in short run
2. Shift in AS curve in long run

Shift in AS curve in short run

In short run some costs are fixed and some are variable. So the increase in prices does not fully reflected in input prices. Short run aggregate supply curve shows relationship between price level and supply of goods and services which producers are willing to provide in the market.

1. **Production cost**: Decrease in cost of production increases the profit margin

for businesses so they are willing to provide more goods and services at given price level. It causes the AS curve to shift forward/rightward.

2. **Wage rate:** A reduction in wage rate also shift the AS curve forward.

3. **Taxes and Govt. subsidies:** Increase in Govt. subsidies and reduction in taxes will shift AS curve forward.

4. **Prices of raw material**: Reduction in raw material prices also reduce production cost and AS curve shift forward.

5. **Future expectations:** If businesses expect an increase in prices in future they tend to increase production and AS curve shift forward.

6. **Exchange rate:** If a country imports raw material and domestic currency appreciates, the imports will become cheaper. As a result they will expand their production. The AS shift forward.

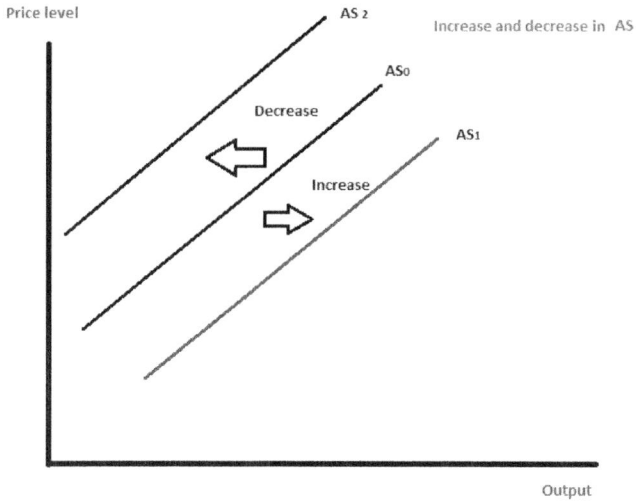

Shift in AS curve in long run

In long run AS curve is perfectly inelastic (vertical) to price level because it is at full employment level of GDP. The factors which can change real GDP can shift long run aggregate supply curve. If these factors increase the real GDP then LRAS curve will shift rightward and vice versa. These factors are as follows;

1.   **Increase/decrease productivity of labor:** If the productivity of labor increases due to any reason, per unit cost of production decreases. The firms would be able to produce more with given units of labor. So the increase in productivity will shift

LRAS curve to right. On the other hand decrease in labor productivity will shift LRAS curve leftward/backward.

2.   **Increase in capital productivity:** Same as labor productivity, changes in productivity of capital will also shift the LRAS curve.

3.   **Increase in supply of labor:** As the LRAS curve shows the output at full level of employment, an increase in labor participation ratio would shift LRAS curve forward.

4.   **Changes in natural resources:** Discovery of new natural resources will also shift the LRAS curve right. Any depletion of existing natural resources would do the opposite.

5.   **Changes in amount of physical capital:** If somehow the physical stock of capital increases (just like labor) the LRAS curve will shift rightward.

6.   **Innovation:** New inventions usually increase the productivity and efficiency of labor and capital. So these innovations can cause the LRAS curve to shift rightward.

LOS 10i: Describe how fluctuations in aggregate demand and aggregate supply cause short-run changes in the economy and the business cycle.

LOS 10j: Distinguish between the following types of macroeconomic equilibria: long-run full employment, short-run recessionary gap, short-run inflationary gap, and short-run stagflation.

LOS 10k: Explain how a short-run macroeconomic equilibrium may occur at a level above or below full employment.

First we need to understand what business cycle is.

Business cycle is the ups and downs in economic activities or real GDP over the time around its growth Trend. A brief description of phases of business cycle is as follows;

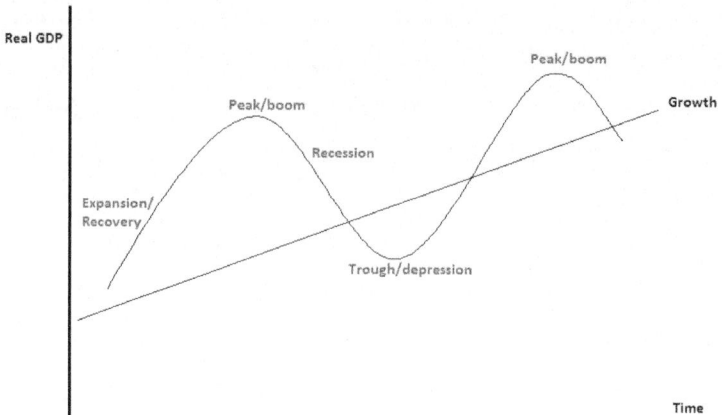

Expansion/Recovery: In this phase of business cycle the GDP is growing while unemployment is getting low.

Peak/Boom: At this stage the GDP is at its highest point. The employment is at its natural level.

Recession: During recession we see a reduction in economic activity like increase in unemployment while reduction in GDP.

Depression: Depression is the stage where economic activities are only nominal. Unemployment is at its highest level and GDP is at its lowest point.

Let's start with the economy functioning at long run full employment equilibrium level.

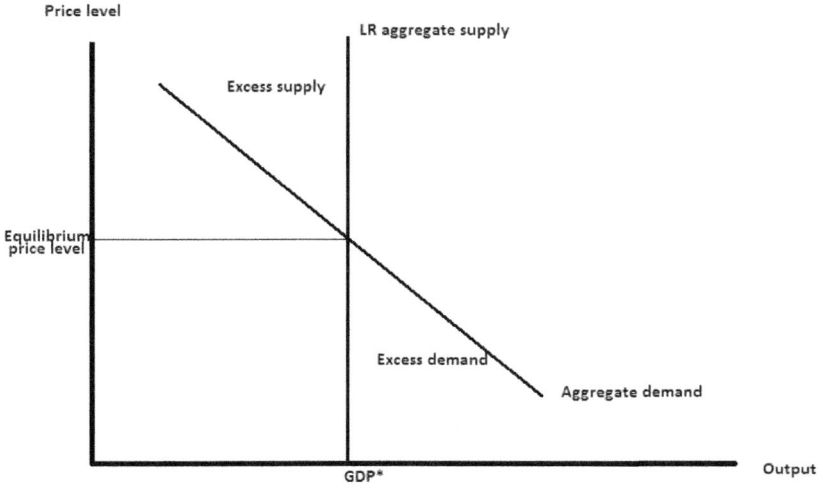

Changes in Aggregate demand

- **Decrease in aggregate demand:** Let's see what happened when AD decreases. Aggregate demand can decrease due to increase in personal taxes, decrease in govt. spending etc. (all the factors which we have discussed before). The effects of reduction in AD can be seen in following diagram.

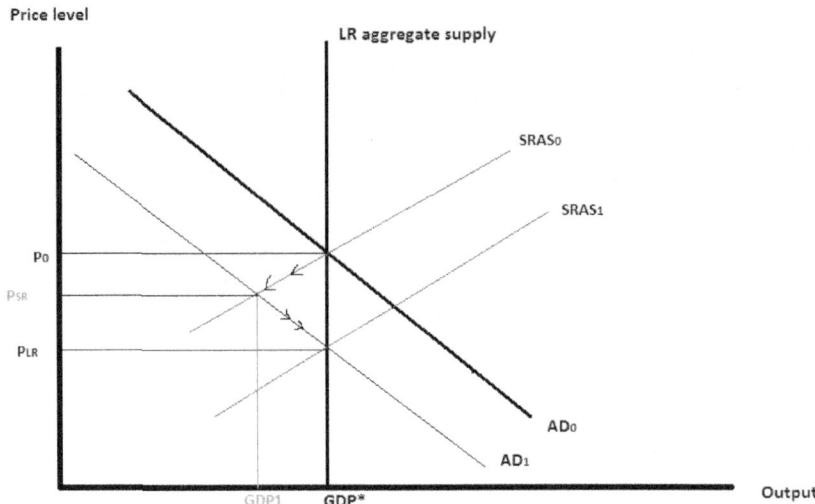

Price level

LR aggregate supply

SRAS₀

SRAS₁

P₀

P_SR

P_LR

AD₀

AD₁

GDP1   GDP*   Output

Initially we are at PO and GDP* which is full employment level of GDP. A decrease in aggregate demand will reduce the price level and real GDP in short run. We will be at PSR and GDP 1. GDP is less than full employment level of GDP this is called recessionary gap. As we have discussed before recession means declining GDP and rising unemployment level. According to classical economist increase in unemployment will reduce the wages as there are more workers competing for the jobs. When the wage rate decreases the labor participation rate also decreases so the short run aggregate supply also decreases from SRAS0 to SRAS1. Due to this the full employment level of GDP will be restored to GDP*. But Keynesians have different point of view. They believe the restoration of full employment level of GDP is long and slow process. Government intervention in the form of expansionary fiscal policy and expansionary monetary policy is desired to increase the aggregate demand and get back to the full employment level of GDP.

- **Increase in Aggregate demand:**

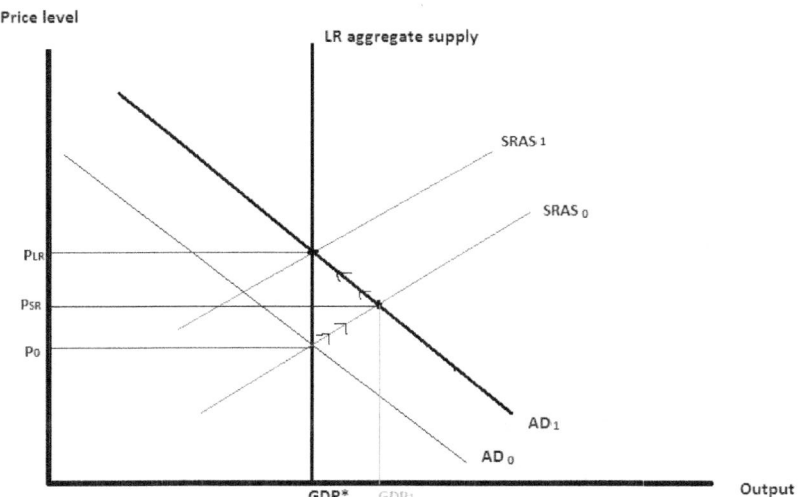

When there is an increase in aggregate demand AD curve will shift from AD0 to AD1 in short run. The new equilibrium level of GDP is GDP 1 and price level is PSR. This GDP1 is higher than full employment level of GDP and PSR is greater than p0. In short run increase in GDP is possible because the workers are working overtime and maintenance of machinery is delayed. This gap between full employment level of GDP and GDP1 is called **_inflationary gap_** because price level is higher now. This level of equilibrium cannot be maintained in the long run. In this scenario the demand for workers and raw materials is increasing so, their prices also Rises. As a result the short run aggregate supply curve will shift backward to SRAS1. With SRAS1 the new equilibrium level is at original GDP level which is full employment level of GDP but we have higher prices PLR now. The net result of an increase in aggregate demand is higher prices only. The government can restore this equilibrium level quickly by decreasing government spending, increasing taxes or decreasing the money supply.

Changes in short run aggregate supply

- **Increase in short run aggregate supply**

Short run aggregate supply can increase due to decrease in input prices.

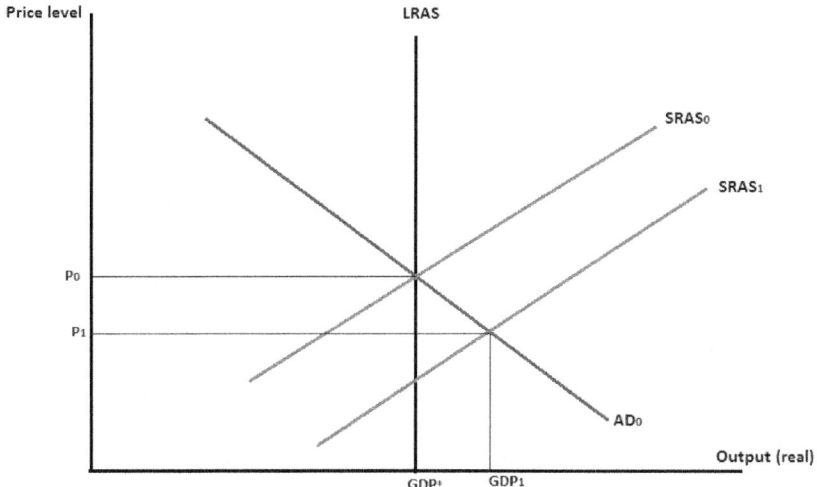

Due to increase in SRAS we have new short run equilibrium at P1 price level and GDP1. GDP1 is higher than full employment level of GDP while P1 is lower price level. In long run when the competition for inputs increases their prices will rise and aggregate supply will shift back to AD0 and original level of price level and full employment level of GDP will be restored.

• Decrease in short run aggregate supply

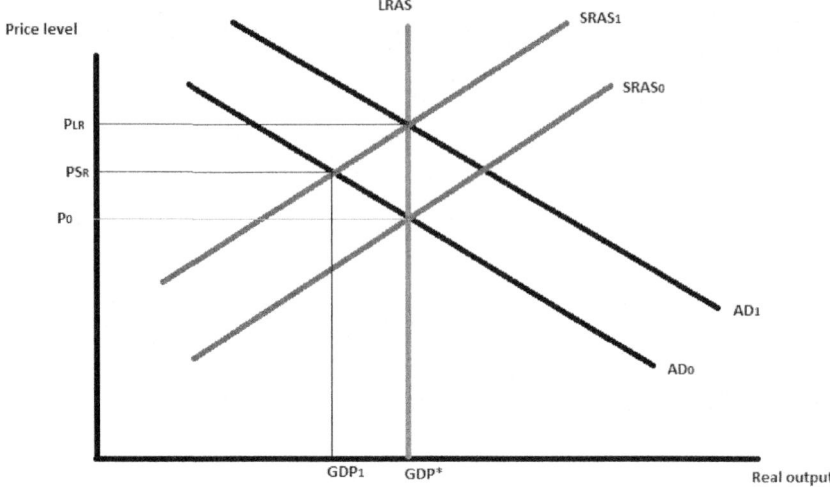

The last case is a decrease in short run aggregate supply. The short run aggregate supply can be decreased due to increase in inputs prices or increase in cost of production. The SRAS1 is the new short run supply curve. Initially we move from GDP* to GDP1 which is lower level of GDP and PSR which is higher price level than P0. This decrease in real output and increase in price level is called **stagflation.** Subsequently decrease in input prices or cost of production will move the economy back to its full employment level of GDP. Full employment level of GDP can also be achieved with expansionary fiscal policy or expansionary monetary policy which will increase the aggregate demand to AD1 and we will be back at GDP* but with the higher price level of PLR.

- Increase in aggregate demand exerts upward pressure on price level while decrease in AD pressurizes the prices downward.
- Increase in aggregate supply exerts the downward pressure on price level while decrease in AS cause the price level to go up.

Increase in Aggregate demand and supply at same time

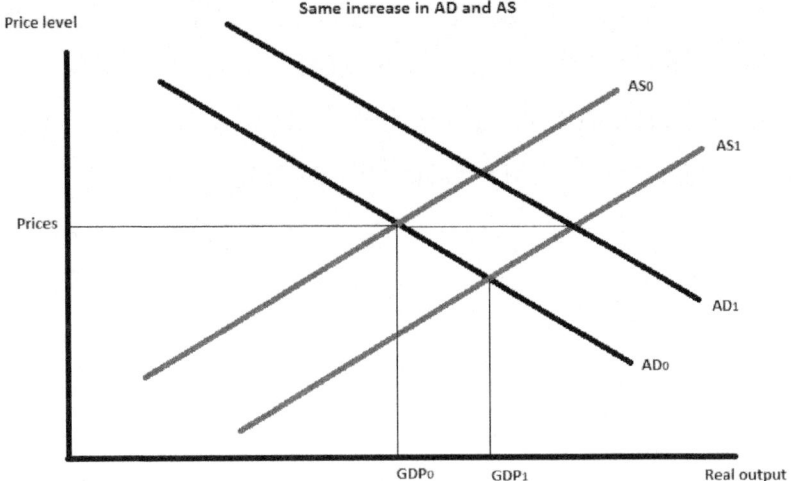

When both aggregate demand and aggregate supply increase, the equilibrium level of output increases. If both increase in same magnitude the price level remains same.
If AD increases more that AS the price level will also rises. And if AS increases more than AD the price level falls.

Decrease in AD and AS

When both AD and AS decreases the output decreases but the price level depends on the magnitude of AD and AS. If AD and AS falls in same magnitude the price level will remain the same as shown in following diagram.

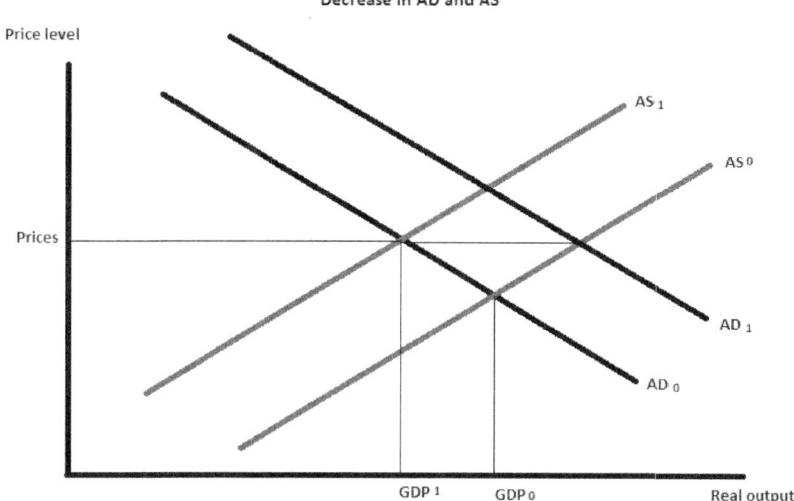

Decrease in AD and AS

Increase in AD while decrease in AS

As we know increase in AD will exert the upward pressure on prices so the price level will rise. On the same time decrease in AS will also make price level to rise. So these two forces are causing the price level to increase as shown in following diagram.

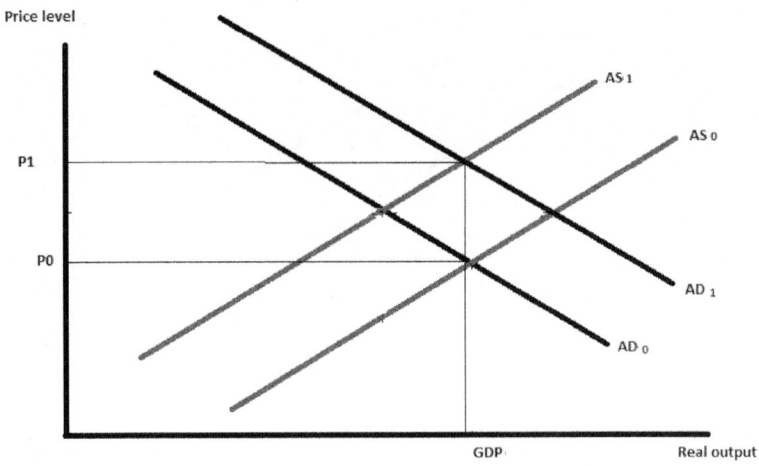

GDP or output level depends on the magnitudes of AD and AS. If both increase and decrease are same then GDP level will remain same only price level will rise.

Decrease in AD and increase in AS

When AD decreases it causes the price level to fall while increase in AS will also make price level to fall. Again overall price level will fall and GDP will remain same if the magnitude of both AD and AS is the same (in opposite directions).

LOS 10m: Describe sources, measurement, and sustainability of economic growth.

Following are some important sources of economic growth.

1.   **Natural resources:** Natural resources like water, oil, coal, iron and other minerals etc. are essential for economic growth. Countries which are rich in these or most of these resources have potential to grow at very fast pace.

2.   **Human resources:** Countries with more labor supply and high quality of skilled labors can grow very fast.

3.   **Physical capital:** Physical capital means factories, machinery etc. More savings leads towards more investment. Investment can cause more physical capital stock. Physical capital increases the efficiency of the labor. As the productivity increases the real GDP increases.

4.   **Technology:** Improvement in technology increases the production efficiency and leads us towards more GDP.

Potential GDP = aggregate worked hours × labor productivity

Growth in potential GDP = growth in labor force + growth in labor productivity

Sustainable economic growth means a rate of growth which can be maintained in long term without causing any other problem in future. Sustainable economic growth is crucial because it is the rate of growth which matters in long run.

LOS 10n: Describe the production function approach to analyzing the sources of economic growth.

Production function means relationship between inputs and outputs. We have two major inputs like labor and capital so in production function we can see output as a function of labor and capital.

Q=A X f (L, K)

Q= total output

A is the productivity of labor or capital also called technological factor.

L= Number or size of labor force

K= amount of available capital

The production function can also be stated as per worker basis;

Divide production function by L

Q/L =A x f (K/L)

Q/L is production or output per worker (average output per worker).

K/L is capital per worker.

This equation tells us that the output can be increased by either of two ways, by improving technology (A) or increasing capital per worker. It means long term sustainable growth can be achieved by increasing labor supply, labor productivity and also by increasing stock of capital.

LOS 10o: Define and contrast input growth with growth of total factor productivity as components of economic growth.

With production function we know that output is a function of inputs.
$Q = A \times f(L, K)$
Growth in potential GDP = growth in technology + WL *(growth in labor)* +WC *(growth in capital)*

WL is percent share of capital in GDP.
WC is percent share of labor in GDP.
The output capacity or potential GDP can be increased by following two factors
1. The accumulation of more inputs like capital raw material and labor.
2. The discovery of new technology and technological advancement.
The growth in labor and capital is called input growth. The increase in output or GDP attributed not towards labor and capital is called total factor productivity. It is the increase in output due to technological advancement and shown in production function with letter A.

READING 11: UNDERSTANDING BUSINESS CYCLES

LOS 11a: Describe the business cycle and its phases.

Business cycle is the ups and downs in economic activities or real GDP over the time around its growth Trend. A brief description of phases of business cycle is as follows;

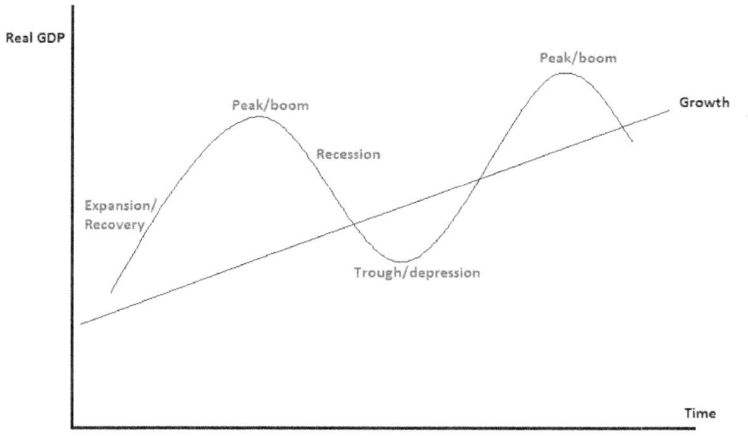

Expansion/Recovery: In this phase of business cycle the GDP is growing while unemployment is getting low and consumer`s spending are increasing.

Peak/Boom: At this stage the GDP is at its highest point. The employment is at its natural level.

Recession: During recession we see a reduction in economic activity like increase in unemployment while reduction in GDP.

Depression: Depression is the stage where economic activities are only nominal. Unemployment is at its highest level and GDP is at its lowest point.

The fluctuations in business cycle vary from some years to decades. The business cycles are most likely to occur in business dominant countries. The agricultural or highly state managed countries are less likely to face a business cycle.

LOS 11b: Describe credit cycles.

The changing availability and cost of credit is referred to as a credit cycle. They depict the expansion of private sector credit, including loan availability and its consumption.

Lenders are more inclined to issue credit and on favorable conditions when the economy is improving. While, in a bad economic situation, lenders' willingness to extend credit will be limited, and the terms will be unfavorable, resulting in a drop in asset value and defaults and economic weakness. Credit cycle is a small part of financial or business cycle.

Applications of credit cycle:
Loose availability of credit to private sector can contribute towards financial crisis. This much availability of credit leads in making of real estate and asset pricing bubbles, which burst when the market realizes it weak fundamentals. Changes in access to external financing also lengthens the recession and other phases of business cycle i.e. expansion and contraction. Although credit cycle goes along with the business cycle, the credit cycle tends to be deeper, longer and sharper than business cycle.

Consequences for the policy: Investors must pay attention to credit cycle stage for the variety of reason such as;

- It help them to understand the changes in housing and construction sectors.

- It also help them to understand the magnitude of business cycle expansion and contraction and what are the policy makers tend to do in each situation.

LOS 11c: Describe how resource use, consumer and business activity, housing sector activity, and external trade sector activity vary as an economy moves through the business cycle.

Resource Use

Inventories are considered very important indicator for business cycle. Businesses try to have adequate inventory in hand for smooth sales operations. When expansion phase of Business Cycle is near to its Boom the sales growth start getting slow. Means inventories are being accumulated. In this scenario inventory to sale ratio is above than its normal level. When businesses see they have more in their storage and sales are not increasing at very high speed they start decreasing their production. Reduction in production by most of the businesses is very important cause of contraction in later period. We know that in calculation of GDP we include inventories in GDP. By seeing only GDP we may expect Economic Strength in future while the economy is going to its contraction.

The aggregate demand decreases more when the firms start to reduce their cost by firing more employees and using less and less capital. With decrease in aggregate demand prices are getting lower and lower. And the economy reaches its trough. At trough the opposite happens. The prices are too low the people start buying more goods and services. As a result the aggregate demand starts to increase. The inventories are getting depleted more quickly and the inventory to sales ratio is lower than normal. To meet the market demand firms start to produce more. They need to hire more capital and labor. This is the economy entering into recovery or expansion again.

Housing Sector

Housing sector follows the trends in business cycle and is correlated with interest rate. Low interest rates encourage the consumers to buy mortgages.

If the future Expectations about the income and the consumer`s wealth is not very good people are not going to buy the mortgages and houses.

If a country has more people between 25 years to 40 years of age they tend to buy more houses and the construction activity increases.

The External Trade Sector

If demand for foreign goods increase the imports increase. Imports are highly dependent upon the domestic cyclical phase while exports depend on the external business cycle phase. If the domestic country is in expansion it demands more goods and services. The imports of that country increases. Near peak level the domestic currency is very much strengthened (with strengthened exchange rate) so the exports become very expensive for other countries. So in this phase imports increases but exports decreases. Due to decrease in the exports the domestic currencies start weakening which will subsequently make exports cheaper for other countries. And demand for domestic exports start to increase.

LOS 11d: Describe theories of the business cycle.

Neoclassical school: Followers of neoclassical school believed that if the economy is deviated from the full level of employment it will move back towards full employment level automatically. They believe if there is a recession in the economy the wage level would go down and this low level of wages and fall in prices of other inputs will encourage the firms to hire more people and other inputs like capital. With more inputs the production level will increase. The "supply creates its own demand" formula will restore the economy back to full employment level of real GDP. According to them the business cycles are temporary and govt. interventions are not required and not desired to restore the economy.

The Great Depression of 1930 supported the theory of new classical economists. Depression was very much prolonged. It took several years to restore the economy back to full employment level.

Austrian School: Economist of Austrian schools believed that the business cycles are caused by the government interventions of increasing the real GDP or employment level. When the government artificially decreases the interest rate in order to increase employment the firms use more borrowed money to invest in long-term businesses. So producing more than the actual demand and when they pile up their inventory in form of finished goods and sales are not happening very much they start to decrease the cost by firing the people. As a result unemployment increases.

Keynesian school: Keynes and his followers called Keynesians, explain the business cycle as shift in the aggregate demand is due to changes in the future Expectations of the businesses. Sometimes the firms over invest and produce more goods and services while the actual demand is not there and when they see their production is not getting sales, they try to reduce the cost and reduce the production level by hiring less and less people. Keynes also argued that the economy will not restore back to its full employment level of GDP automatically. Even if it is restored in the long run it is very slow and painful process. The government intervention is necessary and very much desirable in order to boost the aggregate demand and restore the economy to its full employment level. One argument which Keynesians give is when the economy is facing depression or recession the prices of other inputs decreases while the wages are downward sticky. It means monetary wages cannot decrease from a certain point. This will cause disequilibrium in labor market. This disequilibrium because of sticky wages is a great hindrance in the Restoration of the economy.

The new keynesian school second the above argument and added their two cents as the prices of other inputs are also downward stick like the wages which is another barrier for the economy to restore to its original level.

Monetarist school: The followers of this school believed that the business cycle occurs either due to the external shock or inappropriate monetary policy. They suggest that the rate of growth of money supply should be appropriate and steady and predictable in order to maintain a certain level of aggregate demand.

Neoclassicals come up with the explanation of the great depression in the form of **real business cycle theory.** They argued that deviation from full employment level of GDP is due to the external shocks. Again they believed in no intervention policy as they said the phases of business cycle are efficient market responses to the external shocks.

LOS 11e: Interpret a set of economic indicators and describe their uses and limitations.

We have three types of economic indicators
1. Leading indicators 2.Coincident indicators
3. Lagging indicators

1. **Leading indicators:** Leading indicators are those indicators which may predict the business cycle. Average weekly work hours in manufacturing, new orders for consumer goods and non defense capital goods, housing permits, S&P 500 equity price index, Leading Credit Index, 10-year Treasury to Fed funds interest rate spread, average weekly claims for unemployment insurance and consumer expectations are some major leading indicators. These indicators should be paid special attention because they have the strong tendency to change ahead of Business Cycle.

2. **Coincident indicators:** These indicators changes during the business cycle progression. Real personal income, industrial

production index are some coincident indicators.

3. **Lagging indicators:** Lagging indicators are changed after the economy has entered into a phase of Business Cycle. So these indicators confirm the prediction set by leading indicators. Average duration of unemployment, labor cost per unit, CPI, are some lagging indicators.

Organization for Economic Cooperation and Development (OECD) and Economic Cycle Research Institute (ECRI) publishes indexes for economic indicators for major economies. All these indicators should be analyzed together. If one or two leading indicators change their direction while other leading indicators are not, analyst should not predict a change in economic activities. Beware that these indicators have tendency but not exact relationship with business cycle.

LOS 11f: Describe types of unemployment and compare measures of unemployment.

Three types of Unemployment

1. Frictional unemployment: When people are moving from one job to another or fresh graduates are searching for their first job these people are unemployed temporarily, this type of unemployment is called frictional unemployment. Frictional unemployment cannot be eliminated completely because employers are always expanding or contracting their businesses and people move from one job to another job for better opportunities. This type of unemployment is also referred as natural rate of unemployment.

2. Structural unemployment: When there is a long term structural change in an economy some people are unemployed that type of unemployment is called structural unemployment. For example there is a technological change in the economy which is permanent. People who do not acquire new skills will be unemployed while the people who adopt new technology and new skills will be in demand.

3. Cyclical unemployment: Unemployment caused by business Cycle is called cyclical unemployment. When the economic activities are getting low people become unemployed due to less demand.

Unemployment: Number of people who are not working, are able to work and are actively searching for job, is called unemployment.
Number of people who are seeking for job for several months are called Long Term unemployed.
Labor force: Total numbers of unemployed and employed people are collectively called labor force. So labor force = Employed + unemployed.

Unemployment rate: Percentage of people from labor force who are unemployed is called unemployment rate.
 Unemployment rate = number of unemployed people/total labor force.
People who choose not to be in labor force are **voluntarily unemployed**. They are not included in the calculation of unemployment rate.

Underemployed: Number of people who are working below than their potential, working part time, or working for low paying job despite being qualified for higher paying job are called underemployed.

Participation ratio/ activity ratio/ labor force participation rate: This is the percentage of working age population in the labor force.

Discouraged workers: These are people who are available for work but they are not actively seeking for job. These people are discouraged by trying for several months to get a job but they were unsuccessful. Due to discouraged workers the participation ratio fluctuates.

During depression these workers are disappointed and not seeking for their jobs. When the economy expands these people expect their job hunting will get better results. In this phase firms are hiring more people but these discouraged people are also entering into the labor force. Because of their entrance the unemployment rate does not improve as it should be. That's why we say that the unemployment rate is a lagging indicator for business cycle.

LOS 11g: Explain inflation, hyperinflation, disinflation, and deflation.

Inflation: Persistent increase in general price level is called inflation. General Price level means prices of almost all goods and services. Due to inflation the purchasing power of the currency decreases. Inflation benefits the borrowers while it's a loss for lenders of money.

Inflation rate: Percentage increasing price level is called inflation rate.

Inflation rate
$$= \frac{prices\ at\ current\ time\ -\ prices\ at\ base\ year}{prices\ at\ base\ year} * 100$$

It is the responsibility of Central Bank to control the inflation rate. Central Bank issues monetary policy to control the price level.

Hyperinflation: When the inflation is out of control and the currency is being devalued more than 50% in a month it is called hyper inflation. Hyper inflation exists in the countries with severe crisis like war. This type of inflation destroys the value of money and thus destroys the financial system of a country.

Disinflation: Inflation rate decreasing over a period of time but remains greater than zero is called disinflation. Disinflation is also called negative inflation. It is associated with deep recession when prices are getting too low.

LOS 11h: Explain the construction of indexes used to measure inflation.

To calculate the rate of inflation we construct price index. Price index is a weighted average price of specific basket of goods and services at some specific time. Then we compare the changes in price level with this price index. The most commonly used price index is **consumer price index also called CPI**. It is the best known indicator for price level in US and other countries.
CPI measures weighted average prices of a basket of goods and services which a typical consumer uses like food Medical and transportation etc.

CPI =
$$\frac{Cost\ of\ basket\ of\ goods\ or\ services\ at\ time\ t}{Cost\ of\ basket\ of\ goods\ or\ services\ at\ base\ year} * 100$$

Cost of basket of good at base year: We calculate this by taking prices of specific goods and services (with old prices) which are typical consumer uses and multiply each by its weightage in the household expenditures and add all the results.

Cost of basket of good at current year: We calculate this by taking prices of specific goods and services (with current prices) which are typical consumer uses and multiply each by its weightage in the household expenditures and add all the results.

The weights are given to each good or service according to the typical consumer`s purchasing pattern. Consumers' patterns are different in different countries so the weights might be different in different countries.
There is also difference in Collection of data, sampling of data, the population and also the basket of goods in different countries.
Analysts should know these differences.

Personal consumption expenditures price index (PCE): This index is constructed by taking all the expenditure by household on durable and non durable goods and services. Data for this index and calculation is done by the United States Bureau of Economic Analysis (BEA). This is another alternate for the CPI.

GDP deflator: We have done this in GDP calculation section. This is also a widely used inflation measure.

Wholesale price index/ producer`s price index (PPI): It is the index of basket of goods and services at wholesale rate. This means we are taking the prices for which the producers are selling (not the retailers). WPI can also be used on semi finished products by taking their prices. By doing this the analyst can examine what is causing the prices to increase.

Headline inflation: It the inflation measure used to calculate the inflation for all the products.

Core inflation: It another index which measures inflation by considering all products excluding food and energy. Food and energy products are considered to be highly volatile and sometimes we need to see what non volatile things are doing alone.

LOS 11i: Compare inflation measures, including their uses and limitations.

We have calculated the inflation rate in previous l o s. The method we used was actually **Laspeyres index**.

Laspeyres index = $\dfrac{\Sigma(pc,tn)x\,(qc,to)}{\Sigma(pc,to)x\,(qc,to)}$

This index can be upward biased due to following reasons.

1. *High priced new goods:* In this index we continuously replace older goods for new goods. These new goods initially have higher prices. So adding new goods makes this index upward biased.

2. *Quality changes:* When price of a good increased due to change in its quality or up gradation of a product, this index would show higher prices. But these higher prices are not due to inflation but the product up gradation.

3. *Substitution effect:* Consumers try to substitute the expensive good for their cheaper alternatives. So the statisticians continuously add more weight to those new goods. By changing the weight and adding new products would change the result of this index and make this index less reliable.

Paasche index: This index takes the prices of current year, prices of base year and unlikely laspeyres index, it uses current consumption weight. (The laspeyres index uses current year prices, base year prices and base year's consumption weight).

$$\text{Paasche index} = \frac{\Sigma(pc,tn) x \ (qc,tn)}{\Sigma(pc,to) x \ (qc,tn)}$$

Paasche index remove the upward biasness of laspeyres index but other drawbacks are still there. It may also ads downward biasness which is also a problem.

Fisher index: This is also called ideal price index. It is the geometric mean of laspeyres price index and Paasche price index. This index eliminates the most of the drawbacks of other two indices.

Fisher index = P_f = $\sqrt{}$ (Paache index x Laspeyres index)

Note: In this l o s we are not required to calculate these indices.

LOS 11j: Contrast cost-push and demand-pull inflation.

We have two types of inflation
1. Cost push inflation   2. Demand pull inflation

1. **Cost push inflation:** Increase in price level
   due to increase in the cost of production is
   called cost push inflation. Cost of production
   increases when the prices of inputs like
   wages, energy, raw material is increasing. It
   decreases the aggregate supply.

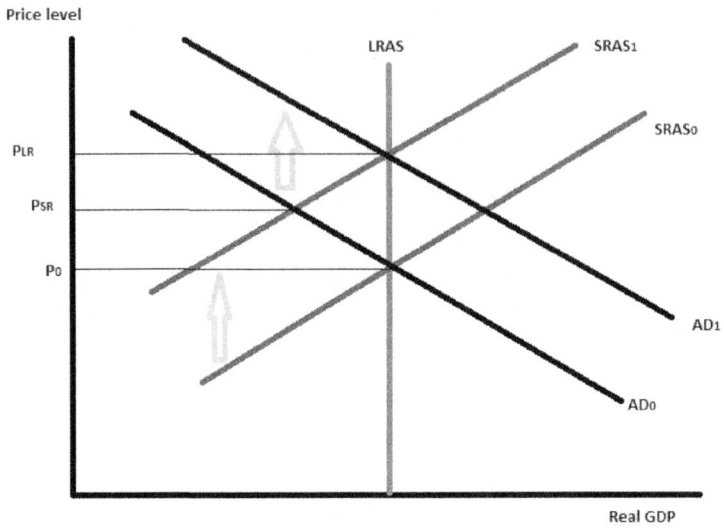

As shown in the above figure, due to increase
in cost of production short run aggregate
supply decreases from SRAS0 to SRAS1.
Due to decrease in SRAS the price level goes
up to PSR which is higher than P0. But we
know that economy will come back to full
employment level of GDP so the AD goes up
and the new price level is even higher than
PSR. We end up having high price level due

to original shock of increase in cost of production and reduction in aggregate supply. This is called cost push inflation. One major source of cost push inflation is increase in wage rate. Usually upward pressure on wage rate occurs when cyclical unemployment is lower than what it should be. But it can also occur when there is cyclical unemployment in the economy but some employees are very crucial for the production process and they cannot be fired even in times of low demand.

Another reason for upward pressure on wage rate is employee`s expectations about inflation rate. When they expect higher inflation they demand higher wages.

2. **Demand pull inflation:** Increase in price level due to increase in aggregate demand is called demand pull inflation. We know that aggregate demand can be increased due to increase in government spending or increasing money supply etc. When economy is at full employment level and aggregate demand increases it only increases price level.

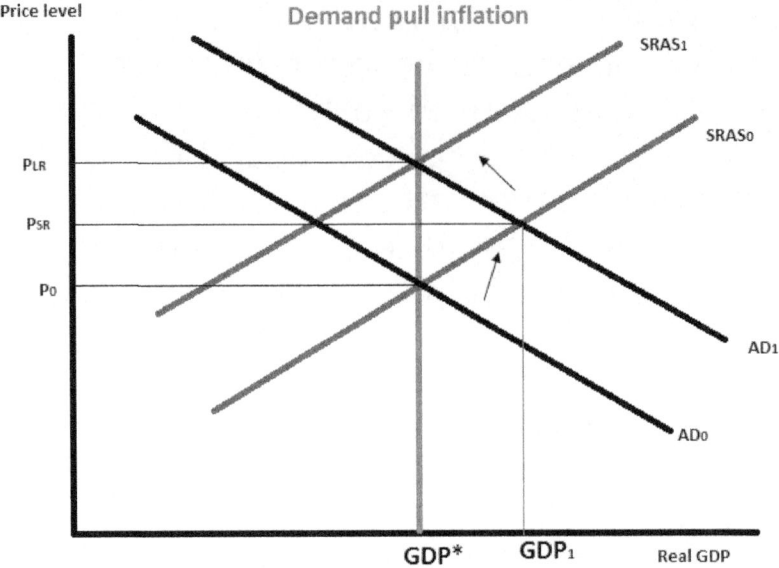

Demand pull inflation

Initially we are at p0 and GDP*. When aggregate demand increases from AD0 to AD1 we get GDP1 and PSR. GDP1 is higher than full employment level of GDP so the real wages will increase. Increase in real wages will cause the short run aggregate supply curve to shift back. We have new equilibrium level for same GDP level (GDP*) with higher prices PLR. This is called demand pull inflation.

READING 12: MONETARY AND FISCAL POLICY

LOS 12a: Compare monetary and fiscal policy.

Monetary policy

This is the policy used by the central bank to affect the quality of money supply and credit in the economy. Central Bank uses this policy to influence economic activities and price level in the economy. So the policy about money and credit supply is called monetary policy.

Expansionary monetary policy: It is also called accommodative or easy monetary policy. When central Bank uses different tools of monetary policy to increase the money and credit supply in the economy that is called expansionary monetary policy.

Contractionary monetary: It is also called tight or restrictive monetary policy. When Central Bank uses the monetary policy tools to decrease the amount of money or credit in the economy that is called contractionary monetary policy.

Fiscal policy

This policy is in the hands of government. Government uses this policy to affect the economic activities and redistribution of wealth. This is the policy about government revenues and government spending (the government budget). The major portion of government revenues is Texas. When the revenues are more than spending the budget is called surplus budget. On the other hand when spending are more than revenues that budget is called deficit budget. When revenues and spending are same or equal that is called balanced budget.

 Expansionary fiscal policy: When spending increases or taxes are lower it is called expansionary fiscal policy.

Contractionary fiscal policy: When taxes are more or spending or less that is called contractionary fiscal policy.

Both of these policies are used by their respective authorities to maintain economic stability, price level, economic growth and wealth distribution.

LOS 12b: Describe functions and definitions of money.

Anything which serves as medium of exchange, store of value and unit of account is called money. Money has three basic functions; medium of exchange, store of value and unit of account.

1. Medium of exchange: Medium of exchange or means of payment is the first and foremost function of money because it is something which is generally accepted as the means of payment for goods and services.

2. Unit of account: It means prices of all goods and services are measured in form of money like dollars, rupees or yen.

3. Store of value: Money can also be used to store the value. We can save the money received to use it for future payments or future consumption.

Narrow money: The amount of currency notes and coins in the circulation and checkable bank deposits are called narrow money.

Broad money: Narrow money Plus all types of bank deposits (other than checkable deposits as they are already included in narrow money) and other assets which can be used for payments (like treasury bills, equity stock and other liquid assets of Gold, Diamond etc).

LOS 12c: Explain the money creation process.

Money creation is a process by which monetary authorities (usually the central bank) increase the money supply of a country or region.

The process of money supply goes back in the early stages of money development when people deposited their precious metals like gold with early bankers. Those bankers issued the more like promissory notes to the depositors (a promise to return the gold to the depositor on demand). When bankers saw these promissory notes are circulating as mean of exchange and nobody is coming back to get his gold back the banks started to lend this gold to earn interest. From here the fractional reserve banking started.

Through this system the banks reserve some amount and lend the unreserved amount. When a bank lends some money the borrower hold some cash in his bank account and spend the rest. The receiver of this cash also deposits the money into the bank. The bank reserves some money from this deposit too and lends the other money. This lending borrowing and again lending process is so continuous the original amount is multifold.

The money can be created from a deposited according to the following formula.

$$\text{Money created} = \frac{New\ deposit}{Reserve\ requirement}$$

For example is $10000 are deposited into bank account and reserve requirement is 10% the money created with deposit would be

$$\text{Money created} = \frac{10000}{10\%} = \$100000$$

The money multiplier can be calculated as

$$\frac{1}{reserve\ requirement} = 1/.10 = 10$$

Actually the original formula of money creation is; New deposit x $\dfrac{1}{Reserve\ requirement}$

The second part is money multiplier.

LOS 12d: Describe theories of the demand for and supply of money.

The amount of currency and financial assets households and businesses want to hold is called demand for money.

People demand money for following three reasons

1. **Transactional demand for money**: The amount of money which is held to meet day to day expenses is called transactional demand for money. Transactional demand for money depends upon the income level (real GDP). When income level raises the transactional demand for money increases.
2. **Precautionary demand for money:** Money held for unseen future incidences and emergencies is called precautionary demand for money. It also depends upon the GDP level and size of the firm. Higher the GDP and size of firm the more demand for precautionary need is.
3. **Speculative demand for money:** Money held to take future investment opportunities is called speculative demand

for money. This demand depends upon the risk factor. More the risk is less investment would be.

The interest rate and money demand

Interest rate (especially short term interest rate) has negative relationship with money demand. If the interest rate is higher cost of holding cash would be higher so the households and firms will demand less money and hold more money in form of interest bearing assets and vice versa.

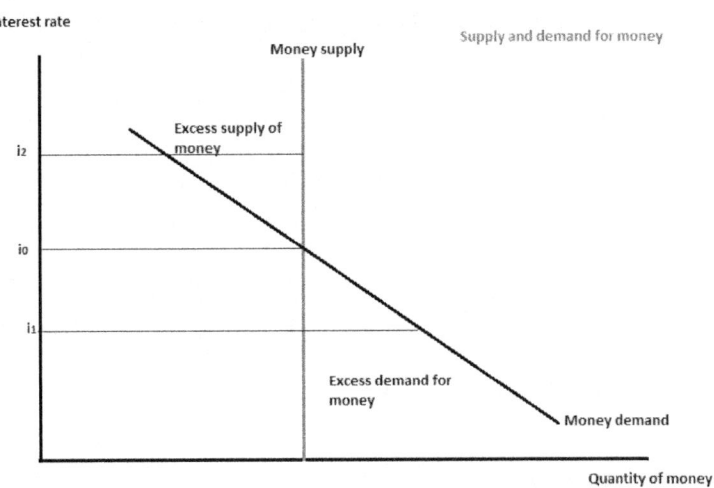

The supply of money is determined by the central bank and is independent of interest rate. While the short term interest rate is determined by the demand for money and supply of money. If the interest rate is above than the equilibrium level there is excess supply of money. It means households and businesses are holding more money than their desire. They will purchase interest bearing securities. When demand for securities will goes up their prices will also goes up and interest rate will fall to equilibrium level. On contrary when the interest rate is lower than equilibrium there would be excess demand for money. People start to sell the interest bearing securities. Selling securities will decrease the securities price and the interest rate will be increased (when price of a security goes down the interest margin will rise) to equilibrium level.

Changes in money supply by central bank

Central bank can also change the money supply in the economy. When central bank increases the money supply it causes the money supply curve to shift forward/rightward. This shift in the money supply curve will pressurize the interest rate to fall as shown in following figure.

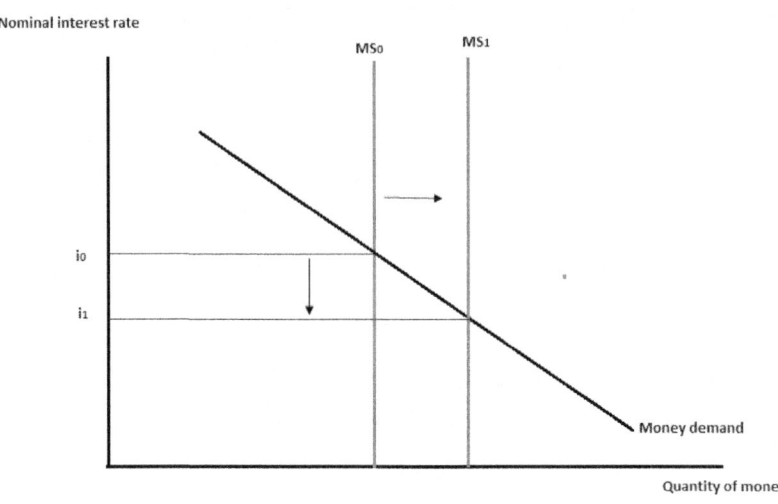

At i_0 there is excess supply of money. Household and businesses have more money than their demand. They will start buying interest bearing securities which will increase the prices of securities and decrease the interest return on these securities. The new equilibrium will be at i_1 interest rate.

The opposite of above can also happen when central bank chooses to decrease money supply.

Note: the central bank can increase (decrease) the interest rate as monetary policy tool but it will not shift the money supply curve but it is called movement along the curve.

LOS 12e: Describe the Fisher effect.

The fisher effect says the nominal interest rate is the sum of real interest rate and expected inflation rate.

This can be expressed in form of equation as follows

$i_n = i_r$ + Expected inflation rate

i_n is nominal interest rate

i_r is real interest rate

This relation can be described in different ways like

Real interest rate is nominal interest rate minus expected inflation.

Expected inflation is the difference between nominal and real interest rate.

The idea behind the Fisher effect is that, real interest rate remains constant and changes in money supply only affect the expected inflation and thus nominal interest rate (money neutrality).

LOS 12f: Describe roles and objectives of central banks.

Following are some major roles of central bank

1. **Issuance of currency:** Central bank is the sole issuer of the currency of a country. No one else can do that. Traditionally the central bank backs some precious metal like gold to issue the currency. Later the banks used to back a reserve of the issued currency by gold, other metals or even foreign reserves to issue currency. Some central banks also issue currency without any

back. That is called fiat money (the legal tender money).

2. **Bank of the government:** Central bank serves as government bank and provides consultation to the government.

3. **Banker of the banks:** The central bank also provides guidelines, regulate and supervise the other banks in the country.

4. **Monetary policy:** It is the central bank that issues and regulates the monetary policy in a country. Through monetary policy it can stabilize price level in country. It has many tools for monetary policy.

5. **Lender of last resort:** Whenever the other banks face shortage of funds due to any reason they can take loans from central bank. Central bank helps them to meet their short term requirement in case of emergencies.

6. **Holder of Gold and foreign exchange:** Central banks also hold foreign reserves and gold for multipurpose.

7. **Payment system regularization:** Central bank makes rules and guidelines in

the country for the safest and secured payment system in the country.

Objectives of central bank

The main objective of central bank is to maintain price stability and target certain level of inflation. As zero inflation rate has never been a good idea for economic growth, maintaining some percentage of inflation has always been a target for the central bank. Inflation rate of 2 or 3 % is considered to be good for the health of an economy. Zero inflation can risk the economy for deflation.

The secondary objectives of Central Bank can be achieving full employment, maintain stability in exchange rate, sustainable economic growth and maintain a certain level of interest rate.

From secondary objectives maintaining a certain exchange rate is of most importance because a volatile exchange rate even when appreciated has certain problems for imports and exports of a country. One method is pegging the domestic currency with most traded foreign currency (like dollar). When dollar is getting higher value than their domestic currency they sell their foreign reserves of dollar to appreciate the domestic currency and vice versa (this act is called pegging). This act can risk increasing or decreasing of money supply.

LOS 12g: Contrast the costs of expected and unexpected inflation.

Expected inflation	Unexpected inflation
It is anticipated inflation by the economic agents like businesses, household, employees	It is the exact inflation above or below than expected inflation
Employees, households and businesses adjust their decisions according to the expected inflation	If the inflation rate is above than expected the borrower of the finances get benefits at the cost of ender. The borrower is paying less than what he borrowed. If the inflation is lower than expected the lender benefit at cost of borrower because he is getting more value when the money is received.
Menu cost and shoe leather costs are	Income inequality and risk premium are

Expected inflation: The inflation which was anticipated by the economic agents like businesses, household, employees etc is called expected inflation. The businesses continuously change their prices accordingly (called menu cost). There is another cost called shoe leather cost associated with this inflation. It is the cost of people holding less cash and having more visits to the bank (actually the opportunity cost).

Unexpected inflation: The inflation greater or lower than what was expected is called unexpected inflation. If the inflation rate is above than expected the borrower of the finances get benefits at the cost of lender. The borrower is paying less than what he borrowed. If the inflation is lower than expected the lender benefit at cost of borrower because he is getting more value when the money is received. One the inflation is greater than what was expected, people always start seeking risk premium.

LOS 12h: Describe tools used to implement monetary policy.

Monetary policy is used by central bank with main objective to stabilize the price level. Following are some tools to implement this policy.

1. **Bank rate/Policy rate/Discount rate:** It is the rate at which the central bank lends money to the other banks in its jurisdiction. If the rate is higher (lower) the borrowing banks` financing cost rises (falls) and the circulation money falls (rises). European central bank calls this refinancing rate.
   Another way to apply this is central bank comes into agreement with other bank to buy their securities at lower price and will resell with higher price. The difference (percentage) is the interest rate (also called effective rate).

2. Reserve requirement: Banks are required to deposit certain percentage of their deposits into central bank. Increasing the reserve rate would reduce the funds available to lend and hence the money supply can be reduced.

3. Open market operation: This is another tool by which the central bank buys and sells the securities in open market. When the central bank wants to increase (decrease) money supply it buys (sells) the securities available in the market. This causes more (less) cash availability with investors and other economic agents and hence more (less) funds are available to lend.

LOS 12i: Describe the monetary transmission mechanism.

Monetary transmission mechanism: This is a process by which changes in monetary policy especially the bank rate affects the price level and economy. Changes in policy rate can be transmitted to the price level and aggregate demand in following four ways

1. Short term interest rate   2. Asset's price

   3. Currency exchange rates   4. Expectations of economic agents

1. **Short term interest rate:** An increase or decrease in policy rate will increase or decrease the interest rates charged by other banks to its clients. Higher (lower) interest rate will lead to less (more) demand for borrowed funds and reduce (increase) the aggregate demand.
2. **Asset's price:** Bonds, equity and other assets' value will decrease (increase) with increase (decrease) of interest rate as discount factor will increase (decrease). When prices of assets decreases people start saving more and consume less (wealth effect).
3. **Currency exchange rates:** Increase in interest rate will attract foreign investment in debt and interest bearing securities which will lead to appreciation of the domestic currency relative to the foreign currency and vice versa. We know that appreciation in domestic currency reduces the exports and it increases the imports.

4. Expectations of economic agents:
With an increase (decrease) in interest
rate households and businesses starts to
consume less (more) because they have
to adjust their decisions accordingly.

**LOS 12j: Describe qualities of effective
central banks.**

The central bank of every country is
responsible for price stability and inflation
control. To perform these duties effectively it
must has following qualities.

1.   **Transparency:** Transparency means
the central bank should publicize their views
about economic environment and issue
inflation reports. The central bank should also
announce the policy rate and also why
central Bank thinks this policy rate is
required. The central bank should also be
transparent in decision making process and
other assessments. This quality of
transparency leads towards credibility.
2.   **Credibility:** The economic agents of a
country must have confidence in the
measures taken by Central Bank to control
inflation. To build this confidence central

bank should have very high credibility. To create a sense of confidence central bank should follow their stated intentions.

3. **Independence:** Central bank is independent if it is free from political influences. If central bank is under the pressure of political parties or government it cannot perform and target inflation effectively. Sometimes Central Bank has to take hard decisions which a government or political party cannot take. During that time if the central bank is influenced by politics it will not go well for the economy.

LOS 12k: Explain the relationships between monetary policy and economic growth, inflation, interest, and exchange rates.

In short run monetary policy can affect the real economic growth, inflation, interest rate and exchange rate. The effects of monetary policy can be described as follows;

Economic growth and aggregate demand
If central bank aims to increase real output it applies expansionary monetary policy. With expansionary monetary policy the interest rate is brought down. When interest rate is

down borrowers are encourage to borrow more money while lenders (the banks) have more fund s to lend. Consequently the money supply increases and more businesses are developed/expanded. Since consumers also avail the opportunity to borrow the overall aggregate demand increases.

The increase in aggregate demand also causes inflation and higher employment level.

Another way to see this is from wealth effect channel. Increase (decrease) in interest rate decrease (increases) the net wealth of the households and business. So they tend to decrease (increase) current consumptions.

Effects on inflation: In order to combat inflation the central bank uses contractionary monetary policy. With this policy interest rates are raised. Consequently the money supply decreases and so does the price level.

Foreign exchange: Domestic higher interest rate can attract foreign investment in interest bearing securities. With foreign investment domestic currency appreciates (other thing held constant) and vice versa.

On the other hand the inflation rate also affects the foreign exchange and we know that monetary policy directly hit the interest rate.

Interest rate targeting: Central bank targets interest rate by increasing or decreasing money supply and monetary growth in the country. Monetary authority increases the money supply when the interest rate is above than desired. On the other hand central bank reduces the money supply when the interest rate in below than required.

Inflation targeting: This is the most common practice and legal requirement in most of the countries. Instead of targeting interest rate the central bank targets the inflation rate usually from 1% to 3% by changing interest rate. We have seen the effects of changes in interest rate on the inflation in monetary policy.

Foreign exchange rate targeting: The exchange rate is also being targeted in most of the economies now-a- days for smooth exports and imports growth. When domestic currency is depreciated in relative to foreign currency (usually dollars) the central bank sells its foreign reserves to appreciate domestic currency and vice versa. This is called pegging. This method also has limitations. For example if the foreign reserves are depleted but still required exchange rate are not achieved. Additionally the foreign reserves are also needed for the foreign payments.

LOS 12m: Determine whether a monetary policy is expansionary or contractionary.

Long term sustainable real economic growth is called real trend rate or trend rate. It is estimated.
Neutral interest rate is the interest rate at which economy grows at its trend rate with stable inflation. This interest rate cannot be observed but estimated by using complex models. This rate provides benchmark for the economist in their monetary decisions.

When policy rate is below (above) than neutral rat the monetary policy is called expansionary (contractionary).
Usually we only analyze the nature of monetary policy by examining the interest rate. If Central Bank lowers (increases) its interest rate the policy is expansionary (contractionary).

LOS 12n: Describe limitations of monetary policy.

Although the monetary policy is used for inflation and money supply control but sometimes it does not produce intended results.

Deflation: In case of lower demand monetary authorities try to boost aggregate demand by lowering the policy rate. But in case of deflation the central bank can lower the interest rate to zero even then the aggregate demand cannot be boosted. Now there is no other option remains with the central bank to increase aggregate demand.

Underdeveloped countries with barter system: In many underdeveloped countries there is large sector especially in rural areas where transactions are being held in barter system. What a central bank and its monetary policy can do where there is no money.

Underdeveloped money market:
Monetary policy is ineffective or less effective in countries where money market is not much developed. For example if there is an economy where there are not stocks, bonds and bills monetary policy cannot play its role.

Most liquid banks: When commercial banks have more funds, it means they are not borrowing from the central bank and the policy rate cannot affect their lending to clients.
Foreign banks also make the monetary policy ineffective. In case of tight monetary policy they withdraw cash from their head offices making the policy rate ineffective.

Money held as cash: When people held more money as cash and less in banks they will less likely to borrow from banks and the policy rate cannot affect them. This practice is very common in underdeveloped and developing countries.

Uncertainty: When economic agents are not sure about the country`s future they prefer to hold more cash. Holding cash makes monetary policy ineffective.

Liquidity trap: Liquidity trap is a situation where interest rate is low and people save more and avoid purchasing bonds in a hope that in future the interest rate will rise. This act makes monetary policy ineffective.

LOS 12o: Describe roles and objectives of fiscal policy.

Fiscal policy means government's expenditures and revenues (mostly taxes) to influence economic activities. When the revenues are more than spending the budget is called <u>surplus budget.</u> On the other hand when spending are more than revenues that budget is called <u>deficit budget</u>. When revenues and spending are same or equal that is called <u>balanced budget.</u>

Expansionary fiscal policy: Expansionary fiscal policy means reduction in the taxes and or increase in the government spending.

Contractionary fiscal policy: Increase in taxes and or reduction in government spending is called contractionary fiscal policy.

Role and objectives of fiscal policy

Expansionary fiscal policy is used to come out of a recessionary period. With this type of fiscal policy government spending is increased and taxes are reduces. Due to increase in government spending the aggregate demand increases. Reduction in taxes also increases the disposable income and the consumer demand increases. Both of these effects increases aggregate demand but budget deficit also increases.

On the same lines to slow the economic growth because the inflation rate is too high the government uses contractionary fiscal policy. This policy reduces the aggregate demand and also the budget deficit.

Fiscal policy can also be used for efficient resource utilization. A reduction in taxes encourages the investment. Moreover the higher taxes can be applied in sectors desired to be discouraged. In this way the resource mobilization and utilization can be optimized.

Fiscal policy also helps in removing income inequalities and disparities. In less developed areas a reduction in taxes helps improvement.

According to Keynesians the fiscal policy can affect the economy when it is operating at full employment level. Monetarists say monetary policy is more effective in inflation and the effects of fiscal policy in this regard are temporary.

LOS 12p: Describe tools of fiscal policy, including their advantages and disadvantages.

Fiscal policy has two broad tools

1. Government revenues 2. Government spending

Government revenues

Government collects its revenues in following forms

Taxes: Government collects taxes to manage state affairs and to influence the economic activities. Government collects taxes in following forms

Direct taxes: These are the taxes deducted directly from the income or wealth. These are wealth tax, income tax, corporate tax, capital gain tax etc. These taxes help redistribution of income.

Indirect tax: These taxes are applied on goods/services. These taxes are levied to encourage/discourage consumption of certain goods/services. These taxes include sales tax, value added tax, excise tax etc.

Tax system is considered to be good if it efficient, simple, sufficient, and progressive.

Government spending

Government spends on a number of goods/services as its fiscal policy tools. Following are major spending heads;

Current expenditures/Non-development expenditures: The routine (day to day) expenses of government are current expenditures. These expenditures are required for smooth and continuous working of the government at its current level. These expenditures are purchase of goods and services useable currently. These expenditures have no future impacts. Salaries of employees, stationary expenses and transfer payments are some examples.

Capital Expenditures/ Development expenditures:

Expenditures to build an asset or to remove a liability are capital expenditures. When governments pay their loan, build dams, roads etc. These are called developmental or capital expenditures. These expenditures are made to increase the future efficiency of an economy.

Advantages of fiscal policy

Boost economic activities: Fiscal policy can boost economic activities in a specific sector or region with reduction of taxes or increase in spending in that sector/region.
Efficient use of scarce resources: If some resources are very limited the government can tax on their uses so only efficient and most productive use of those resources can be increases.
Quick results: The fiscal policy creates more quick results than monetary policy.

Disadvantages
Political misuse: Fiscal policy can be used by politicians and can be ineffective.
Delayed implementation: The application of direct taxes usually takes more time to implement so the results would be delayed.

LOS 12q: Describe the arguments about whether the size of a national debt relative to GDP matters.

When revenues of government are less than expenditures (budget deficit) the government borrows money. One popular way to calculate debt is total debt ratio which is total debt to GDP ratio because taxes (revenues) are linked to GDP. Total debt to GDP ratio must be within a certain limit. A higher of this ratio makes investors less confident about the country and the solvency of the country can be at stake. Public debt may not be always a bad sign depending on the nature of debt.

Arguments in favor of fiscal debt relative to the GDP

1. If the debt is mostly consisted of the domestic borrowings it may not of serious concerns. Domestic borrowings are usually very cheap.
2. If the rate of real growth is greater than debt rate the debt will be depleted gradually. (Growth in taxes due to economic growth >Interest rate). It means the debt is being used for development purposes.

3. During recession if government wants to boost aggregate demand by borrowed spending, the borrowing of funds is not bad. Deficit can take the country out of recessionary period.

Arguments against of fiscal debt relative to the GDP

1. If the government has borrowed from international lenders it may of some serious concern if the debt to GDP ratio is higher.
2. If rate of real economic growth is less that the interest rate then the paying off back of debt would be a problem in future.
3. If the debt is not for development purposes but is used for current consumption and paying back of interest it is of serious concern.
4. If government has borrowed during recession but the country is stuck in recessionary period how the government will pay back the debt.
5. Crowding out effect: If government borrows that means the interest rate will go up. This will reduce the private borrowings and investment decreases.

6. Higher debt leads to higher future taxes so the economic activities can be reduced.
7. More indebted country losses the investor's confident.
8. At time of repayment of debt the government may print more money which can lead towards inflation (printing of new money is used to pay domestic debt).

Fiscal policy has two tools spending and revenues. These tools are used to attain economic objectives. For example in case of recession government decides to increase spending or lower the taxes to boost aggregate demand. With this people has more money and economy gets out of the lower demand and recessionary period. In case of boom period and high prices government increases the taxes or lower spending to decrease the aggregate demand. All these actions in fiscal policy are called discretionary fiscal policy.

Fiscal policy does not necessarily give us the desired results due to following difficulties;

1. _Wrong forecasts:_ If the economic forecasts are not predicted correctly it means policy makers are going to make wrong decisions.
2. _Time lag:_ It may take long time to government to understand the economic changes.
   Fiscal policy is in government's hands. Sometimes it is politicized. Moreover the government has to vote for economic decisions. Meanwhile the economic conditions may have worsened.
   Even after implementation it may takes sometimes to affect the economic indicators to change favorably.
3. _Crowding out:_ The crowding out effect can make fiscal policy ineffective completely.
4. _Deficit financing:_ If government is using expansionary fiscal policy to boost aggregate demand it cannot increase the spending beyond a certain level. Eventually the government has to fill the deficit by foreign, local borrowing or by printing new money. Paying back the financed amount is also a problem and

government has to implement higher taxes in near future or they will print new money. These two actions would worsen the situation ever more.
5. *Stagflation:* In case of stagflation (higher unemployment and inflation) the fiscal policy cannot address both problems simultaneously.

LOS 12s: Determine whether a fiscal policy is expansionary or contractionary.

Expansionary fiscal policy: When spending increases or taxes are lower it is called expansionary fiscal policy. Budget deficit increases or surplus decreases with this type of policy.

Contractionary fiscal policy: When taxes are more or spending or less that is called contractionary fiscal policy. Budget deficit decreases or surplus increases with this type of policy.

LOS 12t: Explain the interaction of monetary and fiscal policy.

Both monetary and fiscal policies can be expansionary and contractionay. With their interaction followings four outcomes are possible.

Expansionary fiscal and monetary policies: With both expansionary policies a great boost in the economy occurs. With lower taxes and higher government spending the businesses would produce more while with lower interest rate the borrowing cost falls and investment increases. Both policies will make higher consumption and use of consumer as well as capital goods. So the unemployment decreases and price level rises.

Contractionary fiscal and monetary policies: The aggregate demand and GDP level will be lower due to contractionary fiscal policy while interest rate rises. Hence the cost of borrowing increases. Consequently public and private sector contracts and the price level falls.

Contractionary fiscal policy and expansionary monetary policy: The interest rate will fall due to expansion in money supply while aggregate demand will partly decrease due to less government consumptions. But the private sector aggregate demand will rise (household and businesses) because cost of borrowing is low. So the net effect would be expansion of private sector. The net effect on GDP could be positive or negative depending on the portion of government and private sector in GDP. If G is more than C plus I the GDP will fall and vice versa.

Expansionary fiscal policy and contractionary monetary policy: This is exactly opposite of above case. The aggregate demand will rise due to higher government spending while the interest rate is high due to tight monetary policy. The private sector (household and businesses) would contract. The net effect on GDP could be positive or negative depending on the portion of government and private sector in GDP. If G is more than C + I the GDP will rise and vice versa.

The net effect also depends on the multiplier effect. Usually the fiscal multiplier is higher than monetary multiplier.

READING 13: INTERNATIONAL TRADE AND CAPITAL FLOWS

LOS 13a: Compare gross domestic product and gross national product.

Gross domestic product (GDP): Market value of all final goods and services produced within boundaries of a country in one year is called gross domestic product.
Within boundaries means those goods and services are included in the GDP which are

produced within a country. Anything produced outside of country even by nationals of a country are not included in GDP of that country. On the other hand if a foreigner is producing goods or services in a country that will be included in the GDP of that country (the main difference between GDP and GNP).

Gross national product: It is the market value of all final goods/services produced by nationals of a country in one year. Anything produced by citizen of a country no matter where in the world, is included in the GNP. So here is the difference. When a foreigner is producing something in a country it is included in the GDP but not in GNP. If nationals of a country are producing something outside of the country that is included in GNP but not in GDP.

Economists are mostly concerned with GDP as it is more related measure of economic activities and employment.

LOS 13b: Describe benefits and costs of international trade.

The benefits

1. **Availability of goods:** With the help of international trade more variety of a specific good is available. Those goods which are not being produced are available to the consumers. So the living standard increases.
2. **Efficient resource allocation:** According to the theory of comparative advantage the countries can allocate their resources for production of those goods/services in which they are most efficient and can import other products. This enables them to allocate their resources more efficiently.
3. **Cost reduction and efficient production:** In order to remain competitive in international market, countries tries to adopt more efficient way of production and reduce their costs. Otherwise they would be out of the market.
4. **Apprehension of shortage can be eliminated:** With more availability of goods the fear of shortage is eliminated.
5. **New markets and international growth:** When goods can be exported internationally the new markets are available for domestically produced goods. Take an example of china. They

have been growing due to their huge share in exports. Also the surplus production can be exported and get revenues. So the fear of overproduction is also eliminated.

Cost or disadvantages of international trade

1. **Political risk:** When a company is mainly exporting to a specific country any changes in politics of that country can harm the exports.
2. **Exchange rate risk:** In imports and exports we are dealing with foreign currencies relative to domestic country. Any change in exchange rate will affect the revenues and trade. For example if domestic currency is appreciated the exports becomes dearer for other countries. And if domestic currency is depreciated the imports become dearer. Also the revenue increases/decreases with changes in exchange rate.
3. **Dependency:** If a country is importing a very sensitive good, crucial for the survival or growth of that county, and the exporting country stops the supply the importer country can be at great

risk. For example imports of oil and Weapons.

4. **Domestic industry can be discouraged:** If a country starts importing a good and its domestic industry is not competitive enough to face foreign competition then the firms will be closed and the people will be unemployed working in that industry. Even if local firms try to compete they need to use capital intensive production methods. This also makes people to lose their job.

Depending on the nature of the country and other policies the international trade can be of greater benefits than being without international trade.

LOS 13c: Contrast comparative advantage and absolute advantage.

Comparative advantage: A country`s (or any entity) ability to produce a good/service at lower opportunity cost is called comparative advantage.

Absolute advantage: A country's ability to produce a good/service at lower per unit cost is called absolute advantage.

Opportunity cost is expressed in the total value of other goods/services which could have produced instead of this specific good/service.
Regardless of existence of absolute advantage international trade is still beneficial if the opportunity costs of different countries are different.

Following example can give us better understanding why the comparative advantage is more important than absolute advantage. This example was given by David Ricardo in 1817. He assumed the world with two countries Portugal and England and two products cloth and wine. Following table shows the Portugal is more efficient (have absolute advantage) in production of both goods but still international trade is beneficial because of comparative advantage.
In the table we see the units of production by each country.

	Yards of cloth	Bottles of wine
Portugal	100	130
England	90	70

Portugal can produce either 100 yards of cloths or 130 bottles of wine with one hour of labor working. The England can either produce 90 yards of cloth or 70 wine bottles with same hours of working labor. According to absolute advantage the Portugal is more efficient and has absolute advantage. But the trade is possible because of difference of opportunity costs.

Opportunity cost of Portugal
Opportunity cost of a yard of cloth =130 / 100 = 1.3 bottles of wine
Opportunity cost of a bottle of wine is 100 / 130 = 0.77 yards of cloth.
Opportunity cost of England
Opportunity cost of a yard of cloth is 70 / 90 = 0.77 bottles of wine
Opportunity cost of a bottle of wine is 90 / 70 = 1.28 yards of cloth.

From above example we can see that the Portugal has lower opportunity cost for producing wine while England has lower opportunity cost for the cloth so Portugal should produce wine while England should produce cloth and trade the other goods.

LOS 13d: Compare the Ricardian and Heckscher–Ohlin models of trade and the source(s) of comparative advantage in each model.

Ricardian model of international trade:
The Ricardo assumed only one factor of production, the labor. He suggested that the difference in cost of production in every country is due to difference in labor productivity caused by difference of technology. This model suggested that every country should produce only that product which it can produce more efficiently.

Heckscher–Ohlin model: This model assumed two factors of production, labor and capital.
This model assumed two goods from which one good (cloth) is capital intensive (more capital is required than labor in production of that good) and the other good (wine) is labor intensive (more labor is required than capital in production of that good). Two countries are assumed from which one country is capital rich (England) and other is labor rich country (Portugal).
This model suggests that the capital rich country should produce capital intensive good while the labor rich country should produce labor intensive good and trade the other goods. This model also suggested that the owner of more available factor of production in each country will gain at the

cost of less available factor. This is because when capital rich country is producing more capital intensive goods (and less labor intensive goods) the demand for capital increases and demand for labor decreases. Same way in labor rich country demand for labor increases and wages will rise and demand for capital will fall (so the reward of capital will fall).

LOS 13e: Compare types of trade and capital restrictions and their economic implications.

Some countries impose trade restrictions. These restrictions are supported by some economists while other economists oppose them. The main reasons to impose restriction are to support infant domestic industries, for national security, and employees' job protection.

Types of trade restrictions

Tariffs: These are the taxes imposed on imports.

Licensing: Licenses are granted to a specific business to import a specific product. Licensing increase the prices of products.

Quotas: These are imposed to limit the amount of imports.

Export subsidies: Subsidies are given to the exporters to encourage exports and make them competitive in international markets.

Content requirement: A restriction imposed by the government that minimum domestic contents must be included in production of a certain product or even a service.

Voluntarily export restraints (VERs): These are the restrictions imposed by exporting country to limit its exports to avoid the import restriction that may be imposed by its importing country. Usually these restrictions are imposed on request of importing partner country.

Economic implications of trade restrictions

We are to examine the effect of each restriction.

Tariff: When tariff is imposed on imports the prices of imported goods rises domestically. Consumption of locally goods increases. So the domestic producer gains while the international producer loses. Government gains from the tariff.

Licensing: Licensing increases the prices while government gains. If licensing is imposed on a product which can be used negatively government can save the society. Again the govt. gains from the licensing fee.

Quotas: Quotas restrict the amount of imports. The domestic consumer lose, international producer lose while the domestic producer gain from it.

Export subsidies: Government provides some subsidies to exporters. The local producers gain as their products are going abroad but local consumers lose as the prices go up. Foreign consumer gains as they have more variety of goods while the foreign producer loses due to competition.

Content requirement: Local producer of those contents gains while the producer of goods is somewhat negatively affected. Foreign and local consumers may be affected by getting somewhat lower quality of goods (if the contents are of high quality they would have been used without any restriction).

Voluntarily export restraints (VERs): The exporter loses while the consumers of foreigner country also lose.

The overall effects of trade restrictions are decrease in consumer surplus, increase local producer's surplus, increase price and decrease quantity of supply.

Capital restrictions

These are the measures taken by the governments to control or restrict the capital outflow. These measures can include the taxes on the income earned by foreign investors, restrictions on excess inflow and outflow of foreign investment, tariffs, volume restrictions etc. These restrictions helps the governments in short run to avoid excessive outflows of capital in recessionary or correction period of domestic country and also to protect domestic newborn uncompetitive industries from foreign competition (foreign more efficient companies are restricted to enter into domestic market by restricting the foreign investment). The consumers lose as the prices goes up while government gains from tariffs. So in long run the costs are more than benefits. But these restrictions are helpful mostly for underdeveloped and developing countries.

LOS 13f: Explain motivations for and advantages of trading blocs, common markets, and economic unions.

There are many trade agreements between countries to reduce trade barriers. These agreements increase the trade among member countries so the overall welfare increases. However trade agreements reduce the trade between non member countries and if member countries are selling dearer goods (than non member countries) the welfare can decrease.

Trading blocs

A trading bloc means some geographically connected nations come together to increase trade and to restrict trade with non member countries.
If they made a free trade agreement it means all restrictions on imports and exports among member countries are removed.
Some agreements also include common type of restriction with non member countries.
Asia-Pacific Economic Cooperation (APEC) and the Association of Southeast Asian Nations (ASEAN) are some examples. These agreements enable the member countries to increase their welfare.

Common markets

All restrictions on imports and exports among member countries are removed.

Member countries adopt a common type of restriction with non member countries.

All barriers to movement of labor and capital among member countries are removed. For example East African Common Market.

Economic Unions

All restrictions on imports and exports among member countries are removed.

Adopt a common type of restriction with non member countries.

All barriers to movement of labor and capital among member countries are removed.

Common institutions and common economic policies are established among member countries.

For example European Union.

Motivations and Advantages

Following can be some motivation and advantages for trading blocs, common markets, and economic unions.

1. Entry into new markets.
2. Increase in the resource availability

3. Future competition can be reduced by gaining competitiveness
4. Reduction of trade barriers.
5. Gain economies of scale.

LOS 13g: Describe common objectives of capital restrictions imposed by governments.

Governments impose restrictions on inflow and outflow of capital to attain following objectives.

1. **Support domestic investment:** Especially underdeveloped and developing countries need to have stable capital accumulation growth by using domestic savings. Foreign investment is considered to be more volatile and can go away in hard times. So countries impose restrictions on foreign investments.

2. **To protect domestic producers:** Foreign companies are usually more competitive than domestic companies (if domestic companies are also competitive there is no need of restrictions). Governments impose these restrictions

to save the domestic producers from getting out of the market.

3. **National security:** Government restricts foreign investment in some strategic areas to secure the country. For example local oil importer or producer is more desirable than foreigner for military to get oil in case of emergencies like war.

4. **Government revenues:** Governments imposes tariffs on foreign investments and capital movements to generate revenues.

5. A haphazard outflow can also create a lot of problems for the domestic country. Government can also reduce these outflows by imposing restrictions.

LOS 13h: Describe the balance of payments accounts including their components.

Balance of payment (BOP): It is systematic record of financial transactions of a country with rest of the world in a specific time period.

It has current account, capital account and financial account.

1. **Current account:** Current account consists of the transactions which are current in nature. It reflects a country's income. It has following subheadings.
   Merchandise: The inflow and outflows of goods come under this heading. Buying and selling of raw material, manufactured goods etc. The net of goods bought and sold is called trade balance or balance of trade (BOT).
   Services: Tourism transactions, technical services etc.
   Income receipts and payments: The dividend income or payment from foreign stocks.
   Unilateral transfers: transferred goods like gifts and aid are also included in current account. (Donor of aid includes it in capital account).

2. **Capital account:** It records the transactions of capital transfer (Financial and non financial assets transfer).It shows the changes in the ownership of assets. This account has two subaccounts
   Capital Transfer: The items like debt forgiveness, transfer of goods and financial assets by the individuals getting

into or going out of the country etc come under this heading.

Sales and purchases of non-financial, non produced assets: This includes intangible assets like patent rights, rights to natural resources, copyrights, trademarks, leases etc.

3. **Financial account:** Also called foreign reserves account. It measures the changes in international ownership of assets. Ownership can be any type like by government or central bank, businesses or individuals. The assets can be of any type like gold and currencies, stocks or bonds and also foreign investments. Financial account has two sub accounts, *Domestic ownership of foreign assets and foreign ownership of domestic assets.*

The net of all these accounts is called balance of payments. If the net is zero we say is there is balance in balance of payments. If we are buying more goods than selling our current account would be in deficit. If buying is less than selling the current account would be in surplus. A deficit in current account is offset by the capital and financial account.

Means if we are buying more it means we are paying by either selling of assets or by getting foreign loan. A current account surplus is also balanced by the financial and capital account. It means we are using our income to build assets or paying loans back. Remember a deficit is not always a bad thing. During initial phase of economic development countries import more capital goods and pay by loan.

LOS 13i: Explain how decisions by consumers, firms, and governments affect the balance of payments.

Decisions by the consumers

When the consumers start to spend more the exports of the country falls (more goods/services are consumed domestically) while imports are increased. It causes a trade deficit. With trade deficit the domestic currency tends to depreciate.

On the other hand if consumers save less but investments are more it means savings are not equal to investment. The excess investment is being financed by foreign loan. This can hit BOP negatively.

Government' decisions

Government's spending also increases the aggregate demand and imports can be increased while exports decrease. Government can also choose to control and manipulate balance of payment by direct control like imposing certain restriction of quotas and import duty to reduce trade deficit. Second tool used by governments is exchange control. Government can depreciate currency to increase exports and make a favorable trade balance.

Firm`s decisions

More demand for capital goods also increases aggregate demand. It can be financed by the domestic or foreign resources. Moreover it causes to increase exports and availability of import substitutions. All these actions make BOP favorable.
Investments by foreign firms increase the capital inflow and hit the BOP positively.

LOS 13j: Describe functions and objectives of the international organizations that facilitate trade, including the World Bank, the

International Monetary Fund, and the
World Trade Organization.

World Bank

World Bank was established in December
1945 to help the devastated countries from
World War II to reconstruct.
World Bank assists its member countries to
promote foreign investment, helps in their
balance of payment issues, provides low
interest loan for short and long run growth
and development projects. They also help the
middle income nations to get out of the
extreme poverty. World Bank also provides
guarantees for the member countries for loan
and foreign investments.

International monetary fund (IMF)

IMF does following for its member
countries

- It promotes international monetary
  cooperation.
- It facilitates the international trade
- It helps to maintain stable exchange
  rate.
- It helps the international payments and
  tries to eliminate payment restrictions.

- Provides short term funds for adjustments in balance of payment.
- It also provides consultation for its member countries.

World Trade Organization (WTO)

According to WTO they do following (more at WWW.WTO.ORG)

The World Trade Organization (WTO) is the only global international organization dealing with the rules of trade between nations. At its heart are the WTO agreements, negotiated and signed by the bulk of the world's trading nations and ratified in their parliaments. The goal is to ensure that trade flows as smoothly, predictably and freely as possible.

READING 14: CURRENCY EXCHANGE RATES

Exchange rate: The value of one currency in terms of another country is called exchange rate. For example 1.15 Dollars for 1 euro. We will write 1.15Dollar per one euro or $1.15/1 € or 1.15 USD/EUR.

In this example the dollars is price currency while euro is base currency. 1.15 dollars is the price of base currency in terms of price currency. The price / base currency is quotation is direct quote for the residents of price currency while this is indirect quote for the residents of base currency.

Nominal exchange rate: Number of units of the domestic currency that can purchase a unit of a foreign currency is called nominal exchange rate. For instance 1.15USD/euro is nominal exchange rate as it tells residents of USA they need 1.15 dollars to buy one unit of euro.

Real Exchange rate: Real exchange rate tells us how many goods/services of domestic country can be exchanged with goods/services of foreign country (while the nominal exchange rate tells us how much domestic currency units can be exchanged with the one unit of foreign currency).

Real Exchange rate = Nominal exchange rate

$$x \frac{price\ level\ in\ base\ currency}{Price\ level\ in\ foreign\ country}$$

For price level we normally use CPI.
Real exchange rate is of more concern with imports and exports than nominal exchange rate. When real exchange rate is high the relative prices of home country are higher than foreign price level. So exports are dearer for other countries while imports are cheaper for the domestic residents. As a result net imports increases. In contrast when real exchange rate falls, net exports increases.

Spot exchange rate: An exchange rate applicable in case of immediate delivery. By immediate delivery mostly means delivery after two days of transaction.

Forward exchange rate: An agreed exchange rate between parties to exchange specific amount of currencies in future date. These forward contracts are of mostly 30 days, 60 days, 90 days, or one year. These contracts are made when a party (or a firm) need a currency in future but fears that the exchange rate will move unfavorably. By getting into forward contract the firm is saving its position against exchange rate risk (also called hedging of risk).

For example a USA firm is entering into contract with a British firm to exchange USD with British pound at a rate of 1.28USD/£.

LOS 14b: Describe functions of and participants in the foreign exchange market.

Functions of foreign exchange market

In absence of foreign exchange market the international trade is almost impossible. Residents of different countries trade goods and services in different countries. For this they need foreign currency which is available in foreign exchange market.

Larger portion of transactions in foreign exchange market is financial market transactions (flow of capital). Investors use foreign exchange market to convert currencies to invest in other countries. When the parties involved in foreign market feels risk (of movement of exchange rate unfavorably) they enter into forward currency exchange contract (as we have discussed in previously). Other contracts of foreign exchange market to hedge risk include foreign exchange swaps (FX swaps), FX options, and outright forward contracts (we will discuss them later in other volume). Some participants try to speculate the exchange rate and purchase some currency (they think is undervalued) and sell it when it appreciates and get benefits.

Participants in the Foreign Exchange Market

The foreign exchange market participants are of two types the buy side and sell side. The sell side is consisted with large multinational banks. On the buy side there are clients of these banks who use these banks to undertake transactions. The buy side participants include following;

Corporations/corporate account: Multinational corporations do business in different countries through FX market. They hedge exchange rate risk by hedging.

Investment account: Parties involve in investment in securities of other countries. They hedge or speculate using currency derivatives. Two broad types of investment account are real money accounts and Leveraged accounts. **Real money accounts:** These are the cross-border investments in mutual funds, pension funds etc. These accounts do not use derivatives. **Leveraged accounts** investment accounts with use of derivatives.

Government: Government also uses FX market for foreign transactions like buying/selling military equipments.

Central banks: Central banks use FX market to maintain a certain level of exchange rate.

They also use foreign currencies to pay the imports bills.

Individuals and small entities:
Households also do FX transactions to convert currencies in order to go to a foreign country they need foreign currency etc. Small entities like tourism firm also need FX market.

LOS 14c: Calculate and interpret the percentage change in a currency relative to another currency.

Let`s say the exchange rate between USD and Euro changed from was 1.15USD/Euro to 1.45 USD/Euro. The percentage change in USD for Euro is calculated as
$\frac{1.45}{1.15} - 1 = 26.08\%$.

It means the Euro is appreciated by 26.08 % relative to USD as it can buy 26.08% more dollars.
It also means that the USD is depreciated relative to Euro but we cannot say the

depreciation in USD is 26.08%. To calculate depreciation in USD we need to convert the quote USD/Euro to Euro/USD. So the initial exchange rate now is 1/1.15 = 0.869 and second quote is 1/1.45 =0.689. Now calculate percentage change as

$$\frac{0.869}{0.689} - 1 = 26.12\%$$

In our example the difference is slight but it can be much more so always calculate the appreciation/depreciation carefully. <u>Always remember we can calculate the percentage change (appreciation/depreciation) of base currency in a quotation.</u>

LOS 14d: Calculate and interpret currency cross-rates.

We can calculate the exchange rate of a currency by using division and multiplication of other exchange rate. This is called currency cross rate of resulting currency. Currency cross rate are used to calculate exchange rate when there is no active foreign exchange market for that currency is available.

For example if we have a quotation of USD/Euro and Euro/CAD then we can calculate USD/CAD as follows;

USD/CAD = USD/Euro x Euro/CAD.
Let's solve with the help of an example.

USD/Euro = 1.15   Euro/CAD = 2
USD/CAD = USD/Euro x Euro/CAD = 1.15 x 2 = 2.3
It means USD/CAD is 2.3. The cross rate 2.3USD per one CAD.
We can invert the USD/CAD to get CAD/USD quotation like 1/ USD/CAD = 1/2.3 = 0.4347

We can also divide two currencies to get desired results.

LOS 14e: calculate an outright forward quotation from forward quotations expressed on a points basis or in percentage terms.

Forward exchange rates are different from spot rates. Forward rates are quoted as difference between spot and forward rates. There are many ways in which forward rates can be expressed and point base is one of them. These points are added or subtracted from the spot rate to get forward rates. When these points are added (subtracted) to spot rate this is called forward premium (discount). The unit of point is the last decimal place in the spot quote rate.

Example

The USD/Euro spot rate is 1.15USD with 6-month forward rate quoted at +2.4 points. What is the USD/Euro 6-month forward rate?

The spot rate is 1.15 so each point of forward rate is 1/100 th . So the forward rate is 1.15 + 0.024 = 1.174. (The forward rate is 0.024 more than spot rate). If the forward rate is negative we would subtracted it.

When the forward rate is given in percentage we simply subtract the percentage from 1 and multiply the result with spot rate.

Example:

Spot rate for USD/Euro =1.15 and the forward rate is 0.032%. Calculate forward rate.

We know 0.032% is 0.00032.

Forward rat = 1.15 x (1-0.00032) = 1.1496

LOS 14f: Explain the arbitrage relationship between spot rates, forward rates, and interest rates.

In freely traded spot and forward currencies contracts, the percentage differences between forward and spot rates are almost equal to the differences between interest rates of two currencies. This is possible due to the existence of arbitrage trades.

An investor has two options to invest
- Invest at domestic risk free rate
- Invest at foreign risk free rate

If the investor chooses to invest domestically she needs domestic currency and at end of the period she will have (1+ id). If she chooses to invest in foreign market she need to convert domestic currency with foreign currency at spot rate and earn (1+if) and then convert is at forward rate to get revenues in domestic currency.

The relationship between these three can be expressed with the help of following formula.

Forward rate = spot rate x $\{(1 + if)/(1 + id)\}$

If the spot rate is greater than forward rate the situation is called **forward discount**. It means the currency will depreciate in coming days. For example if USD/Euro spot is 1.15USD and 3-month forward is trading at 1.10$ the USD is going to appreciate while Euro is going to be depreciated as we are moving to the maturity of forward contract. We will need less USD to buy one Euro.
The Forward premium is opposite to the forward discount. When Spot rate is less than forward rate the situation is called forward premium. For example Spot rate for USD/Euro is 1.15 and 3-month forward rate is 1.20$. This is called forward premium. We will need more dollars to buy one Euro.
The currency with higher (lower) interest rate will be traded at discount (premium) in forward market.

Calculation of discount/premium
Spot rate for USD/Euro is 1.15 and 6-month forward rate is 1.20$. Calculate forward discount/premium.

Forward discount/premium on euro (we calculate this with respect to the denominator currency) = $\dfrac{Forward\ rate}{Spot\ rate} - 1$

$= \dfrac{1.20}{1.15} - 1 = 4.347\%$

This is positive so it is at premium. This is interpreted as the premium on the Euro in forward market is 4.347%.

We can annualize this premium. Since this forward contract is of 6-month so by multiplying by two we can have annualized premium.

LOS 14h: Calculate and interpret the forward rate consistent with the spot rate and the interest rate in each currency.

Using out previous example
USD/Euro spot rate is 1.15$. Annual interest rate of USD is 6% while interest rate of Euro is 9%. What is 1-year forward exchange rate to avoid arbitrage?

We know that Forward rate =Spot rate x $\dfrac{1 + iUSD}{1 + iEuro}$ = 1.15 x $\dfrac{1.06}{1.09}$ = 1.1184

The forward rate is less than spot rate by

$\dfrac{1.1184}{1.15} - 1 = 2.75\%$ which is close to 3% (3% is the difference between interest rate of two countries).

Remember with 1-year forward contract we used annualized interest rate. We need to use six month interest rate with 6-month forward contract by converting it if not available. Also remember that usually the given interest rates are annual rates.

We get forward rate of 1.1184 with no possibility of arbitrage. If the forward rate deviates from this rate there a possibility of arbitrage profit.

LOS 14i: Describe exchange rate regimes.

There are two broad categories of exchange rate regimes. 1. Countries who do have or do not use their own currency 2. Countries with their own currency.

1. **Countries who do have or do not use their own currency**

These countries use either dollarization or are in a monetary union where most of the transactions are done in a common currency.

Dollarization: When a country does not issue its own currency they use the currency of another country. That country cannot own a monetary policy. Ecuador, East Timor, El Salvador are some countries who use dollar and do not have their own currency.

Monetary union: This is a union in which member countries use common currency over their domestic currencies. European Union is the example of monetary union. Each member country cannot issue the monetary policy but participates to determine common monetary policy with European Central bank.

2. **Countries with their own currency**
Following are some practices done by the countries with their own currency.

Currency board arrangement: A board is established which ensures fixed exchange rate. In this arrangement a specific amount of domestic currency is being exchanged with a specific amount of foreign currency.

For example Bulgaria and Hong Kong use this arrangement. Through this arrangement the domestic currency is only issued if it is fully backed by foreign currency like US dollars. These countries cannot manipulate the interest rate and money supply. They usually import interest rate and inflation from foreign currency (backed currency). These countries use their foreign currency to purchase interest bearing securities of foreign currency and earn interest.

Conventional fixed peg arrangement: In this arrangement countries maintain a certain exchange rate (called pegging) with a margin of +-1% with another currency (or basket of major trading currencies like dollar, Euro, Yen etc). These countries issue their own currency, have their own monetary policy so they can manipulate interest rate and inflation. Qatar, Oman, Bahrain use USD to peg the exchange rate.

Target zone: Just like conventional peg but with higher margin of +-2. It gives the countries more flexibility for monetary policy.

Crawling peg: The exchange rate is adjusted periodically usually to adjust for

inflation. It can be active crawling or passive crawling peg. Nicaragua uses crawling peg.
Management of exchange rates within crawling bands: This is the pegging but with margin higher than target zone. This arrangement is used for transition from pegging to floating exchange rate.

Managed floating exchange rates: In this arrangement countries manage their exchange rate with foreign currency (or a basket of currencies) within a wide margin. These countries have their monetary policy and manipulate exchange rate for favorable balance of payment and other indicators like inflation and unemployment. Tanzania, Uruguay, Ukraine use this arrangement.

Free/Independent floating exchange rate: In this arrangement countries do not intervene in determining the exchange rate. Exchange rate is determined by the market forces. Countries with this arrangement only intervene to reduce short term fluctuations. Australia, Canada and Japan are some examples for independent or free floating exchange rate.

LOS 14j: Explain the effects of exchange rates on countries' international trade and capital flows.

When exchange rate changes it affects the quantity and bill of imports. If domestic currency depreciates the goods from other country becomes dearer for domestic residents because they need more domestic currency to buy foreign goods now. As a result imports decreases with currency depreciation. On the other hand if domestic currency appreciates the imports increases.

When domestic currency depreciates the domestic goods become cheaper for the foreigners. So in case of currency depreciations the exports increase and vice versa.

Countries (mostly developing) use this currency depreciation method to decrease the deficit in balance of payment.

When currency depreciates the foreigner investors are attracted as now they need fewer funds to invest. On the other hand appreciation in domestic currency makes somewhat less attraction for the foreign investor.

Elasticity approach: This approach suggests that depreciation in domestic currency only makes balance of payment favorable if the elasticities of imports and exports are greater than one. Elasticity of imports and exports is greater than one if the imports are luxury goods, have more proportion in the expenses and have close substitutes.

J curve suggests that the depreciation will not affect the balance of payment in short run as the payments of import and export goods are normally made in future. But as the time passes the effect of changes in exchange rate start to show its affect. Elasticity approach does not consider capital flow with changes in exchange rate (a drawback of this approach).

Absorption approach: It suggests that when economy is operating less than full employment and currency depreciates the domestic goods/services and assets becomes more attractive and foreign goods/services and assets become less attractive. As a result domestic income and expenditures increases and expenditures on foreign goods/services decrease. Foreigners purchase more domestic assets. Increase in income is more than expenditures. So the balance of payment improves by foreign investment and less imports.

On the other hand if the economy is operating at full employment level (optimal capacity) and currency depreciates the aggregate supply cannot be increased while domestic demand will increase. As a result the price level will increase the imports and exports will go back to its original level (trade deficit), foreign investor will not be attractive to domestic goods/services and it will reverse the effect of currency depreciation on balance of payment.

That's all for the economics. I hope you have enjoyed it. More books are coming in this series. Please review this book as you all did for financial reporting and analysis. Your reviews and suggestions matter a lot to me.

Also checkout our other books on CFA level 1

Financial Reporting and Analysis in one week

Fixed income in one week

Derivatives and Alternative Investments in one week

Printed in Great Britain
by Amazon

41419052R00136